ESL

ENGLISH AS A SECOND LANGUAGE

Beginner

4th Edition

ESL Beginner

ENGLISH AS A SECOND LANGUAGE

Sherry Boguchwal

ESL Skills Consultant
Manalapan, NJ

Johanna Pugni

ESL Skills Consultant
Flushing, NY

Dianne Ramdeholl

ESL Instructor
College of Staten Island — CUNY
Staten Island, NY

Linda C. Robbian

Instructor of Basic Skills
Guilford Technical Community College
Jamestown, NC

Research & Education Association

www.rea.com

Planet Friendly Publishing
✔ Made in the United States
✔ Printed on Recycled Paper
Text: 10%   Cover: 10%
Learn more: www.greenedition.org

At REA we're committed to producing books in an Earth-friendly manner and to helping our customers make greener choices.

Manufacturing books in the United States ensures compliance with strict environmental laws and eliminates the need for international freight shipping, a major contributor to global air pollution.

And printing on recycled paper helps minimize our consumption of trees, water and fossil fuels. This book was printed on paper made with **10% post-consumer waste**. According to the Environmental Paper Network's Paper Calculator, by using this innovative paper instead of conventional papers, we achieved the following environmental benefits:

**Trees Saved: 5 • Air Emissions Eliminated: 966 pounds
Water Saved: 906 gallons • Solid Waste Eliminated: 285 pounds**

Courier Corporation, the manufacturer of this book, owns the Green Edition Trademark.
For more information on our environmental practices, please visit us online at **www.rea.com/green**

Research & Education Association
61 Ethel Road West
Piscataway, New Jersey 08854
E-mail: info@rea.com

ESL Beginner
Premium Edition with e-Flashcards

Printed in the United States of America

Library of Congress Control Number 2012954893

ISBN-13: 978-0-7386-1128-0
ISBN-10: 0-7386-1128-X

Cover image ©iStockphoto.com/mstay

REA® is a registered trademark of
Research & Education Association, Inc.

About Research & Education Association

Founded in 1959, Research & Education Association (REA) is dedicated to publishing the finest and most effective educational materials—including study guides and test preps—for students in middle school, high school, college, graduate school, and beyond.

Today, REA's wide-ranging catalog is a leading resource for teachers, students, and professionals. Visit *www.rea.com* to see a complete listing of all our titles.

Acknowledgments

We would like to thank Pam Weston, Publisher, for setting the quality standards for production integrity and managing the publication to completion; John Paul Cording, Vice President, Technology, for coordinating the design and development of the REA Study Center; Larry B. Kling, Vice President, Editorial, for his supervision of revisions and overall direction; Michael Reynolds, Managing Editor, for coordinating development of this edition; Patricia Karcher and Karen Pica for creating the illustrations for the book; and Weymouth Design and Christine Saul for designing our cover.

CONTENTS

ESL

BEGINNER

CHAPTER 1
Introduction

Chapter 1

INTRODUCTION

ABOUT THIS PREMIUM EDITION

Open a world of opportunity by mastering the English language. REA's *ESL Beginner* with e-flashcards is perfect for beginning-level non-native speakers of English who need to improve their English grammar skills.

The ability to write and speak English effectively is necessary for success in any area, whether it be high school, at work, or in everyday life. English grammar, writing, and speaking skills are a must when applying for a job or advancing in your chosen career. Employers (and their clients) often judge employees according to their ability to communicate precisely and productively.

This book—along with the e-flashcards that come with it—will help you improve your listening, writing, and speaking skills, so you can express yourself in any situation.

Our easy-to-use workbook uses daily living skills to help students understand basic English grammar concepts such as nouns, verbs, simple sentences, compound sentences, and modifiers. Each section contains exercises and examples that let you practice what you have learned as you go. English words that may be unfamiliar are defined for each exercise.

This book is an ideal supplement to textbooks and language courses, and serves as the perfect ESL workbook for anyone learning English.

Whether you're studying English in a class or on your own, this fun and friendly workbook will help you build your skills and communicate with precision.

e-Flashcards: Build Your Word Power

REA's customizable e-flashcards help improve your vocabulary. Study the 450 flashcards included when you buy this book or create your own cards for the words that give you the most difficulty. And because you will create these flashcards through the online REA Study Center (*www.rea.com/studycenter*), you'll be able to access them from any computer or smartphone.

WHO SHOULD USE THIS BOOK?

This book is designed for anyone taking English as a Second Language (ESL) and adult-education classes. A person who is taking an ESL class has grown up in a home where a language other than English is spoken. English-as-a-Second-Language classes teach students how to read, write, and speak English correctly. The classes also teach language skills needed in the workplace and in social settings.

The adult education student is returning to school to review grammar in a basic skills or literacy class setting before entering a GED or Adult High School program. The student may not have completed his or her high school degree or may be seeking a high school equivalency degree based on life experience.

This book may be used by a student who is taking a developmental English class, or it may also be used in a workplace setting to help employees improve their English grammar skills and their job performance.

HOW THIS BOOK IS ORGANIZED

This book is organized into five topics (Chapter 2, "Nouns and Noun Phrases"; Chapter 3, "Verbs and Verb Phrases"; Chapter 4, "Simple Sentences"; Chapter 5, "Compound Sentences"; and Chapter 6, "Modification"). Each chapter is divided into sections (grammar/visualizing pictures, reading, listening, activities, and review). Exercises are included and an answer key ends each section. Below is an explanation of the sections.

Visualizing

This section is divided into two parts: grammar and visualizing pictures. The grammar portion explains the concept to the student. Numerous examples show how the concept is used in a sentence. An explanation follows each example. The visualizing pictures portion shows a picture of daily life in the United States. Images in each picture may be labeled, and there may be a caption under the illustration to help the student understand what is happening. Following each picture, there is an exercise using the grammar concept studied. The following chart lists the grammar concepts and daily life illustrations in each chapter.

Chapter	Grammar	Illustration

2. Nouns and Noun Phrases	Noun (Definition)
	Common and Proper Nouns
	Collective Nouns
	Countable and Noncountable Nouns
	Singular and Plural Nouns
	Possessives
	Phrases
	  –Prepositional
	  –Noun
	Pronouns
		Doctor's Office
		Grocery Store
		Drug Store
		Car Accident
		Ice Cream Shop
		Dental Office

3. Verbs and Verb Phrases	Verbs (Definition) Verb Phrases (Definition) Contractions Subject-Verb Agreement Verb Tense Transitive and Intransitive Verbs	Children's Playground House Trucking Farm Car Repair Garage House Fire

Reading

This section consists of passages that focus on daily life in the United States. Topics include finding a job (chapter 4) and exercise and fitness (chapter 5). A list of vocabulary words and their definitions begin each selection.

Following each passage, there are questions which ask for an open-ended or a specific response, and a grammar exercise that focuses on the concept being studied in the chapter. Each passage ends with a topic for class discussion.

Listening

This section follows the same format as the reading section. A list of vocabulary words and their definitions begin each passage. The conversations are about a situation that a student may encounter in his or her daily life, like a job interview (chapter 4) or placing an order for takeout food (chapter 6). Each passage is followed by an exercise that focuses on the grammar concept studied in the chapter and a topic for class discussion. Students are encouraged to role play the conversations in order to practice their English-speaking skills, or the instructor may read the passages to the class.

Activities

This section allows students to use their new skills in a creative way. The tasks emphasize teamwork to produce a result, such as completing a crossword puzzle (chapter 3) or a word search puzzle (chapter 5) or planning the menu of a new restaurant (chapter 6).

Review

This section begins with a list of key points from the grammar section. It is followed by a series of exercises that focus on the concepts studied.

Students may use the exercises to gauge their mastery of the skills presented in the chapter. Instructors may use the "Review" to test students' skills in a graded or ungraded manner following completion of each chapter.

TO THE INSTRUCTOR

This book and e-Flashcards are based on information gathered from ESL instructors. Grammatical concepts are presented in the context of real-life situations. The book aims to provide students with skills they can use in their daily lives.

Instructional Styles

The instructor may present the material in many ways. He or she may choose to have the class self-paced. This allows the student to progress through the book at his or her own speed. The instructor should work one-on-one with each student during every class meeting to make certain the student understands the material. The instructor may also choose to go through the book with a class as a group. Using this method, everyone studies the same material every class meeting. The instructor may also choose to use a combination of the two instructional styles. The teacher discusses one grammatical concept, such as possessives (chapter 2), or one reading passage each class meeting. Then, he or she allows students to progress through the material at his or her own pace for the remainder of the class meeting.

Instructional Aids

In order to help students better understand the material, the instructor may wish to use props or invite speakers from the community to talk with the class. For example, in chapter 3, "Visualizing," picture b (carpenter), the instructor may wish to bring a hammer to class to show students what an actual hammer looks like, or a restaurant menu for chapter 4, "Visualizing," picture b (restaurant). To help students understand chapter 3, "Visualizing," picture f (firefighter), the instructor may wish to invite the city's fire department educator to speak to the class about the importance of home fire safety.

Providing Feedback to Students

Providing feedback to students is very important. Feedback builds students' self-confidence. The instructor may wish to give the answers to the students or have students check their own work by using the answer key provided at the end of each section. Next, the instructor should discuss missed answers with students. Also, the instructor may wish to provide oral feedback during group work.

Assessing Students' Skills

Many ESL students fear testing and grades. It is important to have graded and ungraded tests and assignments. As the student completes each section, the instructor may wish to place a check mark [✓] in the book or on the sample "Student Progress Sheet," given on the next page, to show work has been completed.

The instructor may wish not to grade chapter exercises but to use the "Review" section at the end of each chapter to assess students' skills as a graded assignment. In addition, the instructor may wish to develop his or her own tests. Testing should be done at the beginning of each class meeting or on designated days.

Creating a Portfolio

Many ESL instructors find it helpful to create a portfolio of each student's writings. This helps the instructor to see each student's progress throughout the semester or quarter. Items which may be included in the portfolio are the "Student Progress Sheet" and, from chapter 3, "Verbs and Verb Phrases," the student-generated sentences in "Visualizing Pictures," (pages 131, 133, 135, 137, 139, and 141), and the writing items in "Activities" (page 167).

Conclusion

The function of the instructor is to teach students how to survive in the classroom, in the workplace, and in a social setting. The instructor should have students read orally to him or her during each class meeting, converse one-on-one with other students, engage students in role-playing conversations, and be an active participant in all class activities. In short, the instructor is the students' lifeline to understanding life in America.

Name: _____   Semester/Quarter: _____

_____   Course Number: _____

STUDENT PROGRESS SHEET

Chapter	Section	Completed
1. Nouns and Noun Phrases		
	Grammar	_____
	Visualizing Pictures	_____
	Reading	_____
	Listening	_____
	Activities	_____
	Review	_____
2. Verbs and Verb Phrases		
	Grammar	_____
	Visualizing Pictures	_____
	Reading	_____
	Listening	_____
	Activities	_____
	Review	_____

3.   *Simple Sentences*

                                    Grammar _____

                                    Visualizing Pictures _____

                                    Reading _____

                                    Listening _____

                                    Activities _____

                                    Review _____

4.   *Compound Sentences*

                                    Grammar _____

                                    Visualizing Pictures _____

                                    Reading _____

                                    Listening _____

                                    Activities _____

                                    Review _____

5.   *Modification*

                                    Grammar _____

                                    Visualizing Pictures _____

                                    Reading _____

                                    Listening _____

                                    Activities _____

                                    Review _____

TO THE STUDENT

Dear Student:

The *ESL Beginner Premium Edition with CD-ROM* will help you improve your English grammar. You will learn how to use nouns, verbs, and modifiers correctly. In addition, you will learn how to write a simple sentence correctly and to form compound sentences. Concepts will be presented in the context of a real-life situation, such as finding a job (Chapter 4, "Simple Sentences") and getting your child ready to enter school in the United States (Chapter 5, "Compound Sentences").

An answer key is located at the end of each section so that you may check your work. Be sure to ask your instructor for help if you miss an exercise item or if you do not understand a vocabulary word or grammar concept. Your instructor is your guide through this book. By using this book, you will gain language skills that will help you in the classroom, in the workplace, and in a social setting.

A chart follows this section. You may use the chart to help you keep track of your progress as you work through this book.

Good luck!

Name: _____   *Semester/Quarter:* _____

MY PROGRESS SHEET

Place a check mark [✓] in the completed column as you finish each section.

Chapter	*Section*	*Completed*
1. Nouns and Noun Phrases		
	Grammar	_____
	Visualizing Pictures	_____

Reading   _____

Listening   _____

Activities   _____

Review   _____

2.   *Verbs and Verb Phrases*

Grammar   _____

Visualizing
Pictures   _____

Reading   _____

Listening   _____

Activities   _____

Review   _____

3.   *Simple Sentences*

Grammar   _____

Visualizing
Pictures   _____

Reading   _____

Listening   _____

ESL

BEGINNER

CHAPTER 2
Nouns and Noun Phrases

Chapter 2

NOUNS AND NOUN PHRASES

GRAMMAR

Noun

A **noun** names a person, place, thing, or animal.

Examples:

Susan Jones (person)

San Francisco (place)

truck (thing)

dog (animal)

Common and Proper Nouns

A common noun names any one person, place, thing, or animal. The first letter of a common noun is not capitalized.

Examples:

girl (person)

park (place)

truck (thing)

dog (animal)

A proper noun names one specific person, place, or thing. The first letter of a proper noun is capitalized.

Examples:

Susan Jones (person)

San Francisco (place)

Statue of Liberty (thing)

Proper nouns include the following:

Personal Names:

Susan Jones

Dr. Harrison

Professor Saunders

President Clinton

Nationalities:

Mexican

Vietnamese

Laotian

Religions:

Buddhism

Hinduism

Baptist

Geographic Names:

Mexico

Vietnam

Japan

Seine River

Pacific Ocean

Holidays:

Thanksgiving

Christmas

Months of the Year:

February

December

Days of the Week:

Monday

Friday

NOTE:

1. The table below shows the difference between a common noun and a proper noun.

	Common	**Proper**
Personal Name:	father	Bob Jones
Geographic Name:	country	Japan
Religion:	church	Baptist
Holiday:	holiday	Easter
Month:	month	July
Day:	today	Wednesday

2. The seasons (winter, spring, summer, and fall) are not proper nouns. The first letter should not be capitalized.

Collective Nouns

A **collective noun** describes a group of people or things considered as a single unit. Some collective nouns are:

audience	band	bunch
chorus	class	committee
congress	faculty	family
gang	flock	government
group	jury	orchestra
personnel	staff	team

Countable and Noncountable Nouns

A **countable noun** is a thing that a person can count.

Examples:

corn (A person can count ears of corn.)

lettuce (A person can count heads of lettuce.)

A **noncountable noun** is a thing a person cannot count.

Examples:

dust (A person cannot count grains of dust.)

grass (A person cannot count blades of grass.)

EXERCISE A: Label each word that is a noun by writing noun (N) in the blank provided. The first one has been done as an example for you.

___N___   1. river

_____   2. run

_____ 3. water

_____ 4. eat

_____ 5. cow

_____ 6. home

EXERCISE B: Label the following nouns as being a common noun or a proper noun by writing common noun (CN) or proper noun (PN) in the blank provided. The first one has been done as an example for you.

__CN__ 1. lake

_____ 2. Monday

_____ 3. United States

_____ 4. church

_____ 5. Atlantic Ocean

_____ 6. day

EXERCISE C: Label the following nouns as being countable or noncountable by writing countable (CT) or noncountable (NCT) in the blank provided. The first one has been done as an example for you.

__NCT__ 1. milk

_____ 2. tree

_____ 3. flower

_____ 4. cereal

_____ 5. jewelry

_____ 6. movie

Singular and Plural Nouns

A **singular noun** names one person, place, thing, or animal.

Examples:

Tom Cope (one person)

Triangle Park (one place)

pillow (one thing)

horse (one animal)

A **plural noun** names more than one person, place, thing, or animal. A plural noun is made by adding "s" after the last letter in a singular noun.

Examples:

Singular	Plural
boy (one person)	boys (more than one person)
park (one place)	parks (more than one place)
pillow (one thing)	pillows (more than one thing)
horse (one animal)	horses (more than one animal)

Some singular nouns form their plurals in special ways.

1. If a singular noun ends in "y," change the "y" to "i" and add "es" to the end of the noun to form the plural.

   Examples:

Singular	Plural
lady	ladies
country	countries

2. If the singular noun ends in "s," "z," "ch," "sh," or "x," add "es" to the end of the noun to form the plural.

   Examples:

Singular	Plural
class	classes
box	boxes
church	churches

3. If the singular noun ends in "f" or "fe," drop the "f" or "fe" and add "ves" to the end of the noun to form the plural.

   Examples:

Singular	Plural
wife	wives
life	lives
leaf	leaves

4. If the singular noun ends in "o," add "s" or "es" to the end of the noun to form the plural.

   Examples:

Singular	Plural
potato	potatoes
piano	pianos

NOTE: If a singular noun refers to music, add an "s" to the end of the noun to form the plural. A "piano" is a musical instrument. Add an "s" to the end of "piano" to form the plural "pianos."

---

5. Some singular nouns change spellings to form their plural forms.

   Examples:

Singular	Plural
child	children
man	men
goose	geese
foot	feet
ox	oxen
mouse	mice

6. Some nouns stay the same in both singular and plural forms.

    Examples:

Singular	Plural
deer	deer
sheep	sheep

NOTE:

1. A noncountable noun stays the same in both the singular and plural forms.

    Example:

    deer (singular), deer (plural)

2. The words "a" and "an" are always followed by singular nouns.

    Examples:

    a cat (singular)

    an elephant (singular)

3. The words "all," "both," "few," "many," "some," and "several" are always followed by plural nouns.

    Examples:

    few days (plural)

    some toys (plural)

4. If a student has a question about the way a plural noun is formed, the student should check his or her dictionary.

EXERCISE D: Change the following singular nouns to plural nouns. The first one has been done as an example for you.

Singular	Plural
1. bird	birds _____

2. sheep   _____

3. tooth   _____

4. baby   _____

5. table   _____

6. wolf   _____

EXERCISE E: Complete the following sentences by using the singular or plural form of the word in parentheses. The first one has been done as an example for you.

1. I bought two __books__ (book) on cooking at a yard sale.

2. A _____ (student) at Central High School won the Brooks Scholarship.

3. Some _____ (vegetable) can be served hot or cold.

4. My two-year-old daughter dropped an _____ (egg) on the kitchen floor.

5. Joyce's son goes to preschool three _____ (day) a week.

6. Many _____ (person) become citizens of the United States each year.

Possessives

A singular noun can be made to show possession by adding an apostrophe and an "s" to the end of the noun.

Examples:

the girl's dress (The girl owns the dress.)

Diana's grades (The grades belong to Diana.)

If the noun is plural, add an apostrophe after the "s."

Examples:

two boys' bicycles (The bicycles are owned by the two boys.)

the girls' dresses (The dresses are owned by the girls.)

If the noun ends in "s," add an apostrophe after the "s" or an apostrophe and an "s."

Examples:

Charles' gloves or Charles's gloves

the princess' gown or the princess's gown

EXERCISE F: Make the following nouns possessive. The first one has been done as an example for you.

1. dog   _____dog's_____

2. man   _____

3. thieves   _____

4. churches   _____

5. brother   _____

6. manager   _____

EXERCISE G: Rewrite the following sentences to make the underlined part show possession. The first one has been done as an example for you.

1. <u>Charles car</u> was stolen.

   Charles' (or Charles's) car was stolen. _____

2. <u>John mother</u> lives in Charleston, South Carolina.

   _____

3. Acme Exteriors is painting <u>James house</u>.

   _____

4.   The safety report showed the <u>truck tires</u> were worn.

_____

5.   I borrowed the <u>secretary dictionary</u>.

_____

6.   Three <u>students science experiments</u> won awards at the city science fair.

_____

Phrases/Prepositions

A phrase is a group of words that makes a sentence more interesting. There are several types of phrases.

Prepositions are connecting words; they connect the word or words that follow them (called the object of the preposition) with some other part of the sentence. A **prepositional phrase** begins with a preposition and ends with the object of the preposition (noun). Some common prepositions are:

about	by	on
across	down	over
at	for	through
behind	in	with
beside		

Example:

John works in an office.

In an office is a prepositional phrase. *In* is a preposition. *Office* is the object of the preposition (noun).

A **noun phrase** can be used as the subject of the sentence or it can be used as an appositive to describe another noun.

Examples:

My lost wallet was found.

My lost wallet is a noun phrase. It is the subject of the sentence.

A Moravian star, a type of outdoor decoration, is popular at Christmas.

A type of outdoor decoration is a noun phrase used as an appositive to describe Moravian star.

EXERCISE H: Underline the prepositional phrases in the following sentences. Label each preposition (P) and each object of the preposition (OP). The first one has been done as an example for you.

P   OP

1. Recently, I read a book <u>about the American Revolution</u>.

2. I live on Northfield Street.

3. I went to the movies with James.

4. The Smiths live across the street from my mother.

5. Su Wong got a job at the bank.

6. I told my boss I would see him at 8:00 in the morning.

Pronouns

A **pronoun** takes the place of a noun. A pronoun can be used as the subject of a sentence or as the object of a verb or a preposition, or to show ownership (possession).

Examples:

Tom likes roses. He bought some for his sister.

In the first sentence, *Tom* is a noun. *Tom* is the subject of the sentence. In the second sentence, *he* is a pronoun. *He* replaces *Tom* as the subject of the sentence.

Tom gave her roses.

Tom gave her roses.

Her is a pronoun. *Her* is the object of the verb *gave*.

Tom gave the roses to her.

Her is a pronoun. *Her* is the object of the preposition *to*.

Tom lost his wallet.

His is a pronoun. *His* shows the *wallet* is owned by *Tom* (possession).

The word to which the pronoun refers is called the **antecedent**. The antecedent may be a noun or a pronoun.

Examples:

Tom bought roses for his sister.

His is a pronoun. *His* refers to the antecedent *Tom*.

He bought roses for his sister.

He and *his* are pronouns. *His* refers to the antecedent *he*.

See Appendix D for more information.

The following charts show singular and plural pronouns and the nouns they replace.

	Singular		
	Noun	**Pronoun**	**Example**
First person:	the writer	I	I like pizza.
Second person:	the person written to	You	You like pizza.
Third person:	another person written about	He, she, it	He likes pizza. She likes pizza. It likes pizza.

Plural

	Noun	Pronoun	Example
First person:	the writer and another person	We	We like pizza.
Second person:	a group of people	You	You like pizza.
Third person:	the writer and a group of people	They	They like pizza.

The following charts show singular and plural pronoun forms and their uses.

Singular

	Subject	Object	Possession
First person:	I	me	my, mine
Second person:	you	you	your, yours
Third person:	he she it	him her it	his her, hers its

Plural

	Subject	Object	Possession
First person:	we	us	our, ours
Second person:	you	you	your, yours
Third person:	they	them	their, theirs

EXERCISE I: Underline the pronoun(s) in the following sentences. The first one has been done as an example for you.

1.   Sally said <u>she</u> would accept the job.

2.   We are going to take our citizenship test tomorrow.

3.   Is that computer disk yours?

4.   Bill left his books in the library.

5.   They said they would paint their new house white.

6.   We are going to see our grandmother tomorrow.

EXERCISE J: Draw an arrow from the pronoun to its antecedent. The first one has been done as an example for you.

1.   My sister said she would feed the cat.

2.   The dress shop is having its winter sale.

3.   Did you lose your credit card?

4.   Susan Wong is taking her daughter to the doctor.

5.   I have my American history class at 11:00 in the morning.

6.   The Garcia family said their children were playing at Oak Hollow Park.

EXERCISE K: Underline the correct pronoun in parentheses. Refer to the pronoun chart on page 29–30 if you need help. The first one has been done as an example for you.

1. (I, Me) will attend Brevard College in the fall.

2. Thomas carried (him, his) nation's flag at the Winter Olympics.

3. Louise said the notebook belonged to (her, she).

4. (We, Our) bus departs at 2:00 in the afternoon for Detroit, Michigan.

5. I am going to watch the movie. (Its, It) looks interesting.

6. I love dogs, but (my, me) husband does not like (them, their).

NOUNS AND NOUN PHRASES—GRAMMAR

ANSWER KEY

Exercise A:

1. N   3. N   5. N   6. N

(Note: Exercise items 2 and 4 are verbs.)

Exercise B:

1. CN	2. PN	3. PN
4. CN.	5. PN	6. CN

Exercise C:

1. NCT	2. CT	3. CT
4. CT	5. CT	6. CT

Exercise D:

1. birds	2. sheep	3. teeth
4. babies	5. tables	6. wolves

Exercise E:

1. books	2. student	3. vegetables
4. egg	5. days	6. people

Exercise F:

1. dog's	2. man's	3. thieves'
4. churches'	5. brother's	6. manager's

Exercise G:

1. Charles' (or Charles's) car was stolen.
2. John's mother lives in Charleston, South Carolina.
3. Acme Exteriors is painting James' (or James's) house.
4. The safety report showed the truck's tires were worn.
5. I borrowed the secretary's dictionary.
6. Three students' science experiments won awards at the city science fair.

Exercise H:

     P   OP
1. about the American Revolution

     P   OP
2. on Northfield Street

     P   OP   P   OP
3. to the movies, with James

       P   OP   P   OP
4. across the street, from my mother

     P   OP
5. at the bank

     P OP   P   OP
6. at 8:00, in the morning

Exercise I:

1. she
2. We, our
3. yours
4. his
5. They, they, their
6. We, our

Exercise J:

1. My sister said she would feed the cat.

2. The dress shop is having its winter sale.

3. Did you lose your credit card?

4. Susan Wong is taking her daughter to the doctor.

5. I have my American history class at 11:00 in the morning.

6. The Garcia family said their children were playing at Oak Hollow Park.

Exercise K:

1. I   2. his   3. her
4. Our   5. It   6. my, them

VISUALIZING PICTURES

Doctor's Office

The doctor is examining a patient.

1. patient
2. doctor
3. woman
4. train

5. monkey
6. desk
7. stepping stool

8. name tag
9. examining table
10. stethoscope

A doctor's office is a place where a person goes to get a checkup or to be healed if he or she is sick. When a person goes to the doctor, the person is called a patient. A doctor helps a person maintain good health and makes a sick person well.

Doctor and office are common nouns. Other common nouns in the picture are train, patient, monkey, desk, name tag, examining table, and stethoscope. Dr. Smith is a proper noun. It is the name of a specific doctor.

EXERCISE: Write a sentence using the following common nouns identified in the picture. The first one has been done as an example for you.

1. boy

   The little boy is crying.

2. woman

3. desk

4. monkey

5. stepping stool

6. train

Grocery Store

The woman reaches for a can of peas.

1. shelf

2. grocery cart

A grocery store is a place where people buy food. Grocery store is a common noun. Other common nouns in the picture are shelf, grocery cart, peas, green beans, corn, lima beans, cereal, bread, and milk. A+ Foods is a proper noun. It is the name of a specific grocery store.

EXERCISE: Write a sentence using the following common nouns shown in the picture. The first one has been done as an example for you.

1. corn

   The cans of corn are on the third row.

2. milk

   _____

3. cereal

   _____

4. peas

   _____

5. lima beans

   _____

6. grocery cart

   _____

Drug Store

The pharmacist helps the woman with her medicine.

1. lab coat
2. counter
3. sign
4. bandages
5. note pad
6. pen
7. medicine bottle
8. purse

A drug store is a place where a person buys medicine. A drug store is a common noun. A pharmacist is a person who fills prescriptions that are ordered by a doctor for a person who is sick. Other common nouns in the picture are lab coat, counter, sign, bandages, note pad, pen, medicine bottle, and purse. Elder Drug Store is a proper noun. It names a specific drug store.

EXERCISE: Write a sentence using the following common nouns identified in the picture. The first one has been done as an example for you.

1. lab coat

   The pharmacist is wearing a lab coat.

   _____

2. counter

   _____

3. medicine bottle

   _____

4. pen

   _____

5. note pad

   _____

6. bandages

   _____

Car Accident

The paramedics treat the accident victims.

1.	ambulance	3.	rubber glove	5.	bandage
2.	car	4.	first aid kit	6.	traffic light

A paramedic helps a person who has been hurt in an accident. A paramedic is a common noun. Other common nouns in the picture are rubber gloves, ambulance, car, first aid kit, bandage, and traffic light. First Street is a proper noun. It is the name of a specific street.

EXERCISE: Write a sentence using the following common nouns identified in the picture. The first one has been done as an example for you.

1. rubber gloves

    The paramedics wear rubber gloves.
    _____

2. ambulance

    _____

3. car

    _____

4. first aid kit

    _____

5. traffic light

    _____

Ice Cream Shop

Hong serves ice cream.

1. banner
2. hairnet
3. bowl
4. ice cream cone
5. ice cream scoop

An ice cream shop is a place that serves different flavors of ice cream like vanilla, chocolate, strawberry, chocolate chip, and rocky road. The different flavors of ice cream are common nouns. Other common nouns in the picture are hairnet, apron, banner, bowl, ice cream cone, and ice cream scoop. Yum Yum Shop and Maytown Ice Cream are proper nouns. Yum Yum Shop is the name of a specific place. Maytown Ice Cream is the name of a specific type of ice cream.

EXERCISE: Write a sentence using the following common nouns shown in the picture. The first one has been done as an example for you.

1. hairnet

   Hong wears a hairnet.

2. banner

   _____

3. apron

   _____

4. bowl

   _____

5. ice cream cone

   _____

6. ice cream scoop

   _____

Dental Office

The patient is learning how to care for his teeth.

1. light
2. toothbrush
3. toothpaste

4. hand mirror
5. dental chair
6. false teeth

7. dental floss
8. smock

A dental office is a place where a person goes to receive care in order to have and keep a healthy mouth. A dental hygienist, dentist, and dental assistant care for the person.

A dental hygienist cleans a person's teeth and teaches a person how to care for his or her teeth. A dentist is a special kind of doctor who fixes a broken tooth, takes out a tooth that is not healthy, and cares for a person's teeth and gums. A dental assistant helps the dentist provide care for a person. A person goes to a dental office two or three times a year to have his or her mouth checked and his or her teeth cleaned. A person also goes to a dental office any time he or she has a tooth that hurts.

Dental office, dentist, and dental hygienist are common nouns. Other common nouns in the picture are light, toothbrush, toothpaste, hand mirror, dental chair, false teeth, dental floss, and smock.

EXERCISE: Write a sentence using the following common nouns identified in the picture. The first one has been done as an example for you.

1. dental chair

    The man is sitting in the dental chair.
    _____

2. toothbrush

    _____

3. false teeth

    _____

4. hand mirror

    _____

5. light

    _____

6. smock

    _____

Discussion:

Discuss ways medical care differs in your country from the United States.

NOUNS AND NOUN PHRASES—
VISUALIZING PICTURES

ANSWER KEY

Doctor's Office
Exercise:

Answers will vary.
Here are some examples:
1. The little boy is crying.
2. The woman is standing next to the boy.
3. The desk is cluttered.
4. The doctor has a monkey.
5. The stool is for small children.
6. The train is painted on the wall.

Grocery Store
Exercise:

Answers will vary.
Here are some examples:
1. The cans of corn are on the third row.
2. The milk is in a carton.
3. The cereal is in the grocery cart.
4. The peas are above the green beans.
5. The lima beans are below the corn.
6. The woman is pushing the grocery cart.

Drug Store
Exercise:

Answers will vary.
Here are some examples:
1. The pharmacist is wearing a lab coat.
2. The pharmacist is standing behind the counter.
3. The medicine bottle has a label.
4. The woman is buying the pen.
5. The notepad is on the counter.
6. The box of bandages has a picture.

Car Accident

Exercise:

Answers will vary.

Here are some examples:

1. The paramedics wear rubber gloves.
2. The ambulance has 911 painted on it.
3. The car is damaged.
4. The first aid kit is open.
5. The traffic light is red.

Ice Cream Shop

Exercise:

Answers will vary.

Here are some examples:

1. Hong wears a hairnet.
2. The banner lists ice cream flavors.
3. Hong's apron is clean.
4. The bowl is on the counter.
5. Hong is holding the ice cream cone.
6. Hong uses the ice cream scoop to put ice cream in the bowl.

Dental Office

Exercise:

Answers will vary.

Here are some examples:

1. The man is sitting in the dental chair.
2. The dentist is holding the toothbrush.
3. The dentist shows the man the teeth.
4. The man is holding the hand mirror.

READING

Topic 1: Home Remedies

Vocabulary

adventurous—liking excitement

approach—way, to come near

cold or flu—an illness or infection that causes a person to have a runny nose, sore throat, body aches, or a cough

cure or remedy—treatment to end an illness

firmly—strongly

fever—an increase of a person's body temperature

indigestion—upset stomach, stomach pain

insomnia—when a person cannot go to sleep

irritates—to make a bad condition worse

pharmacy—a store that sells medication

popular—used by many people

realize—to understand fully

Sometimes, when we are ill with a cold, a fever, or the flu, we go to our doctor for help, or we get some medicine from the pharmacy. Now, many people are beginning to realize that the cure may be in their kitchens!

Many people with colds firmly believe in hot chicken soup for clearing their head and nose. While some people rub oil on their chest, others take a more adventurous approach, mixing red peppers, hot water, lemon juice, sugar, and milk.

Here are some popular home remedies:

Burns. Put the burn under cold water, and then apply some toothpaste on it. Ice usually irritates the burn.

Coughs. Take some honey and lemon juice, and wear very thick socks.

Indigestion. Drink water and baking soda or any hot sweet liquids, like tea.

Insect bites. Wash the sting or bite. Put garlic and orange peel in a wet cloth, and then put it on the bite for 30 minutes.

Insomnia. Drink warm milk and have a warm bath.

EXERCISE A: Answer true or false to the following statements by writing T (true) or F (false) in the blank provided.

_____ 1. Honey and vinegar help a cold.

_____ 2. Ice helps burns.

_____ 3. Baking soda or hot sweet tea is good for indigestion.

_____ 4. Toothpaste usually irritates the burn.

_____ 5. A warm bath helps you go to sleep.

EXERCISE B: Identify the following words and phrases as being a noun, pronoun, or prepositional phrase by writing N (noun), P (pronoun), or PP (prepositional phrase) in the blank provided. The first one has been done as an example for you.

__P__ 1. we

_____ 2. doctor

_____ 3. from the pharmacy

_____ 4. their

_____ 5. for 30 seconds

_____ 6. milk

EXERCISE C: In your native country are home remedies used? Are they similar or different to the ones listed above and on the previous page? Explain.

Discussion

Do you think home remedies are a good idea? Why, or why not?

Write about a popular or interesting home remedy used in your native country.

Topic 2: Conversation Topics

Vocabulary

attack—to speak negatively (badly) about something

boring—not interesting

discuss—speak about

films—movies

hobbies—things people do in their free time

interrupt—to break in

personal—private, something you do not want to discuss with another person

polite—showing good manners (for example, being kind or thoughtful to guests is polite)

stranger—someone whom you do not know very well

In the United States, when two people are meeting for the first time, the topics they usually discuss are family, work, vacations, hobbies, and the weather. They ask questions like: "Where do you work?", "What good films have you seen recently?", "Do you like studying in America?".

These are polite, safe questions. They are not private.

However, there are topics that are personal and, therefore, are not polite to discuss with someone you do not know very well.

You should not ask someone how much money he or she makes from his or her job or how old someone is (especially a woman). It is also not polite to interrupt a person while he or she is speaking.

You should not ask two people who are living together and romantically involved "Why don't you get married?". Also, you should never attack a stranger's ideas or beliefs.

Always remember, what is true in your culture may not be true in someone else's.

EXERCISE A: Decide if the following questions and statements are *polite* or *not polite* by writing P (for polite) or NP (for not polite) in the blank provided.

1. I think your ideas are very boring and stupid. _____

2. How much do you earn per year? _____

3. How old are you, Mrs. Kim? _____

4. Do you like going to the movies? _____

5. Did you watch the NBA game on TV? _____

6. Why don't you two get married? _____

EXERCISE B: Look at the items in Exercise A again. Are they polite or not polite in your native country?

Give two examples each of questions that would be considered polite and not polite in your native country.

Discussion

Do you find the idea of polite and impolite conversation strange? Explain using personal examples.

Go over the story underlining all nouns and noun phrases. Exchange with the person sitting next to you and discuss your answers.

Topic 3: Divorce

Vocabulary

announced—told

counselor—a person who helps by giving advice or suggestions to another person (this is an occupation)

divorce—legal separation of husband and wife

given up on—lose hope

rarely—not often

suddenly—quickly

Bob and Alice met when they were in college in 1980 and got married in 1985. They have a five-year-old son. For ten years, they had a happy marriage. Then, suddenly, after ten years of marriage, Bob and Alice announced to their families that they were getting a divorce.

You are the marriage counselor. Study each story carefully, and then give your advice.

Bob Jones, age 35, computer programmer, $45,000 a year
Bob's statement:

It seems as if Alice has suddenly given up on me. I know I'm not the most exciting person. I work long hours, and we rarely seem to go out to movies and parties anymore. I try to give her support whenever I think she needs it, but she just pushes me away, emotionally. It seems as if our only choice is a divorce.

Alice Jones, age 30, librarian, $30,000 a year
Alice's statement:

Bob and I rarely talk anymore. Whenever he talks, it seems as if he's doing it because he has to, not because he wants to. We're not friends anymore; I think he's stopped seeing me as a woman. He now only sees me as his wife, and we just don't have fun anymore. Tommy (our son) doesn't know about our problems, but I'm afraid he'll find out. I love Bob as a person, I'm just not in love with him anymore.

NOTE: Wherever possible use nouns and noun phrases in your answers.

EXERCISE A: As their marriage counselor, what advice would you give to:

1. Bob? (Give three suggestions he could follow to help improve his marriage.)

2. Alice? (Give three suggestions she could follow to help improve her marriage.)

EXERCISE B:

1. Why do you think the divorce rate is steadily increasing?

2. Do you think divorce would be a good idea in Alice and Bob Jones' case? Explain your answer.

3. Is the number of divorces increasing in your country? How do you explain this?

Discussion

How do you feel about the idea of divorce? Do you think that it can be a good idea? How can it affect the children involved? Compare marriage in America and your native country. Is it different or similar? Explain and give examples.

Topic 4: Tipping

Vocabulary

bellhop—a person who carries luggage in hotels

bill—money that is owed for a service

porter—a person who carries luggage

tip—money given in exchange for a service (for example, in America, a person leaves a tip for the server [waiter or waitress] in a restaurant)

typically—usually

valet—a person who parks your car at a hotel, restaurant, etc.

What exactly is a tip?

It is money a customer leaves to show he or she is pleased with the service in that place. Americans typically leave a tip for servers at restaurants, porters at airports and hotels, hair stylists in hair salons, and take-out food delivery people. One reason why people tip is because those who work in these places are often paid very poorly.

Hotel bellhops usually receive a dollar for each suitcase. A parking valet also receives about a dollar for parking each car. The usual tip for other types of service—for example, hairdressers, waiters and waitresses—is between 15 and 20 percent of the check, depending on how happy the customer is with the service.

In most cases, the bill or check does not include the tip. However, for large groups dining at a restaurant, the tip may be included in the bill.

There is no tipping in cafeterias or fast-food restaurants like McDonald's and Burger King.

EXERCISE A: How much should you tip? Write your answer in the blank provided. If you should not tip, write *no* in the blank provided.

1. Someone who takes your order at McDonald's?   _____

2. A waiter in a nice restaurant?   _____

3. Your hairdresser or barber?   _____

4. A cab driver?   _____

5. A hotel maid who cleans your room?   _____

6. Someone who takes the dirty dishes off the table
    in a cafeteria?   _____

EXERCISE B: What tip should you leave for the following? Write your answer in the blank provided.

1.   A $100.00 restaurant check?   _____

2.   A $25.00 cab fare?   _____

3.   A $43.00 haircut?   _____

Discussion

Is tipping necessary in your country? Do you tip for similar or different things? Explain and give examples. How much do you usually tip in restaurants? Taxis? Hotels?

NOUNS AND NOUN PHRASES—READING

ANSWER KEY

Topic 1: Home Remedies
Exercise A:

1. F   2. F   3. T
4. F   5. T

Exercise B:

1. P   2. N   3. PP
4. P   5. PP   6. N

Exercise C:

Answers will vary.

Topic 2: Conversation Topics
Exercise A:

1. NP (Do not attack someone's ideas.)
2. NP (Do not ask how much a person earns.)
3. NP (It is not polite to ask a person's age, especially if the person is a woman.)
4. P (Hobbies are safe and polite.)
5. P
6. NP (This is personal and should not be asked.)

Exercise B:

Answers will vary.

Topic 3: Divorce
Exercise A:

Answers will vary.

Exercise B:

Answers will vary.

Topic 4: Tipping
Exercise A:

1. No (A tip is not required in a fast-food restaurant.)
2. Between 15 and 20 percent
3. Between 15 and 20 percent
4. Between 15 and 20 percent
5. Approximately $1.00 per day
6. No (A tip is not required in a cafeteria.)

Exercise B

1. Approximately $20.00
2. Approximately $5.00
3. Approximately $8.00

LISTENING

Topic 1: Directions

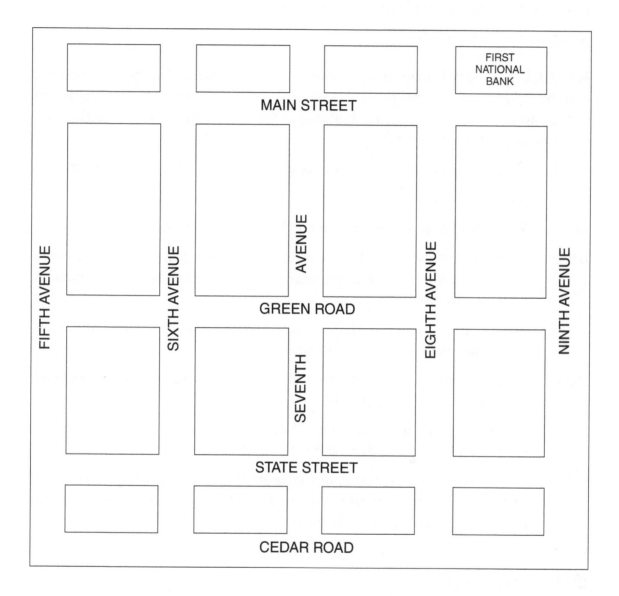

Vocabulary

bookstore—a place where a person can buy a book

grocery store—a place to buy food (a grocery store is also called a supermarket)

hospital—a place that cares for sick people

neighborhood—the area that surrounds your home

neighbor—a person who lives next to you

post office—a place to mail letters and packages

wondering—thinking

EXERCISE A: Jack Rhodes has just moved to Oak Grove and is trying to find his way by asking his new neighbor. Listen as your teacher or a partner reads the conversation. Mark and label each building as you hear it mentioned. The first one has been done as an example for you.

JACK: Hi, Bill. I was wondering if you could help me out with some directions.

BILL: Sure, go ahead.

JACK: Well, the first thing I need to find is First National Bank.

BILL: Well, that's easy. Go right and walk about four blocks to Ninth Avenue, and then turn left. Keep going until you get to Main Street. The bank is on your left, on the corner.

JACK: So, it's on the corner of Main Street and Ninth Avenue on my left. Great. And what about the grocery store?

BILL: Yes, that's pretty important. Well, that's on the corner of State Street and Seventh Avenue, on your right.

JACK: Great! There are just three more places I'd like to ask you directions to - the hospital, the post office, and the bookstore.

BILL: The hospital is on the corner of Cedar and Eighth, on your right. The post office is between Green and Main on Sixth Avenue, on your right, and the bookstore is right opposite the bank.

JACK: Thanks so much. I really appreciate it.

BILL: No problem.

EXERCISE B: Listen as your teacher or partner reads the directions again and complete the following sentences. The first one has been done as an example for you.

1.   First National Bank is on the corner of <u>Main Street</u> and <u>Ninth Avenue</u>.

2. The grocery store is on the corner of _____ and _____ .

3. The hospital is on the corner of _____ and _____ .

4. The post office is between _____ and _____ .

5. The book store is opposite the _____ .

EXERCISE C: List the five places to which Jack wants directions. The first one has been done as an example for you.

1. First National Bank _____

2. _____

3. _____

4. _____

5. _____

Discussion

Give your partner directions to the supermarket, library, or one of your favorite restaurants in your neighborhood. Your partner should then draw a quick map and identify the locations you gave to see whether he or she understood the directions. Reverse roles.

Describe your neighborhood to your partner. Do you like living there? Why, or why not?

Topic 2: Groceries

Vocabulary

clerk—a person who works in a store

pound—a unit of measurement

Listen as your teacher or partner reads the following conversation taking place in a grocery store.

BETSY: I'll have some biscuits and a pound of pasta, please.

CLERK: Anything else?

BETSY: Let's see. I'd also like some bananas. How much are they?

CLERK: They're $1.99 per pound.

BETSY: I'll have a pound, please.

CLERK: Okay. Would you like anything else?

BETSY: Yes, I need some meat, milk, and coffee. How much will this be?

CLERK: That will be $7.50.

EXERCISE A: Look at the picture, and place an X next to the items that Betsy bought at the store.

EXERCISE B: Underline the noun(s) in the following sentences from the passage. The first one has been done as an example for you.

1. I'll have some <u>biscuits</u>.

2. I'll have a pound, please.

3. I'd also like some bananas.

4. They're $1.99 per pound.

5. I need some meat, milk, and coffee.

6. Would you like anything else?

EXERCISE C: Answer true or false by writing T (true) or F (false) in the blank provided. The first one has been done as an example for you.

_____ 1. The bananas are $1.99 per pound.

_____ 2. Betsy bought some coffee.

_____ 3. The total bill came to less than $10.00.

_____ 4. Betsy needs rice and milk.

_____ 5. Betsy bought lettuce and garlic.

Discussion

Answer the following questions in pairs.

1. Compare food prices in your country and in the United States.

2. Which foods in the picture are your favorite? Least favorite?

Topic 3: Lost and Found

Vocabulary

co-worker—a person who works with you

department store—a big store selling many items (Macy's and Wal-Mart are examples of department stores)

lose—to end up without

unimportant—not important

wallet—a folding case where you keep your money and ID cards

Listen as your teacher or partner reads the following conversation between two co-workers.

ANN: Thank goodness for lunch. I thought the phone was never going to stop ringing.

JANE: I know, Ann, it seems as if people never stop losing things. First, John's gloves, and then Ed's notebook and Maggie's wallet.

ANN: Oh, I know, and doesn't Charles ever get tired of dropping his keys? Not to mention Connie and her scarf.

JANE: Oh, I know. I feel as if we're a department store sometimes. Anyway, what did you buy for lunch?

ANN: A cheeseburger, fries, and a Coke. What did you get, Jane?

JANE: I got a salad, soup and yogurt at the deli. Do you want to eat here in the office or go to the park? It's not too cold today.

ANN: The park, definitely. Oh, by the way, is this yours?

JANE: Oh no! This must have fallen out of my purse. Thank you so much. Can you imagine what would have happened?

EXERCISE A: Listen as your teacher or partner reads the conversation again. Circle the items that are mentioned as being lost. The first one has been done as an example for you.

(gloves)

sunglasses

keys

shoes

scarf

tie

EXERCISE B: Answer true or false by writing T (true) or F (false) in the blank provided. The first one has been done as an example for you.

___F___   1. Ann's lunch included a soup and salad.

_____   2. They work in a department store.

_____   3. Jane got her lunch in a deli.

_____   4. Jane lost something unimportant.

_____   5. Ann likes cheeseburgers.

_____   6. They usually eat lunch together.

EXERCISE C: Rewrite the following phrases to show possession. The first one has been done as an example for you.

1. the notebook of Ed

   Ed's notebook
   _____

2. The wallet of Maggie

   _____

3. The keys of Charles

    _____

4. The scarf of Connie

    _____

5. The fries of Ann

    _____

6. The salad of Jane

    _____

Discussion

Answer the following questions in pairs.

1. Do women usually work in your country? What type of positions do they hold? (for example, doctors, secretaries, lawyers, etc.)

2. Do you think the job of the two women in the dialogue seems difficult? Why, or why not?

3. Is it difficult for women working in your country? How? Explain.

4. Have you ever had a job? Describe your experience to the class.

Topic 4: Restaurant

Vocabulary

dressing—used with a salad to make it taste better

to go—customer will take the food to eat it at home or work, etc.

to stay—a customer will eat in the restaurant

Listen as your teacher or partner reads the following conversation heard in a restaurant.

WAITER:	May I take your order please?
CUSTOMER (female):	Yes. I'd like a double cheeseburger, large fries, and a salad.
WAITER:	What kind of dressing would you like?
CUSTOMER:	What do you have?
WAITER:	We have blue cheese, Italian, ranch, and French.
CUSTOMER:	I'll have blue cheese.
WAITER:	What would you like to drink?
CUSTOMER:	I'll have an iced tea.
WAITER:	Is this to stay or to go?
CUSTOMER:	To stay. Thank you.

EXERCISE A: Answer the following questions true or false by writing T (true) or F (false) in the blank provided. The first one has been done as an example for you.

___T___ 1. The customer is not having a potato salad.

_____ 2. The customer eats vegetables only.

_____ 3. The restaurant does not serve dressings with its salads.

_____ 4. The woman is going to have soda to drink.

_____ 5. The woman is going to eat in the restaurant.

_____ 6. The restaurant in the dialogue is probably a fastfood restaurant.

EXERCISE B: Underline the pronoun in the following sentences from the passage. The first one has been done as an example for you.

1. May I take your order please?

2. I'd like a double cheeseburger, large fries, and a salad.

3. What do you have?

4. We have blue cheese, Italian, ranch, and French.

5. I'll have blue cheese.

6. What would you like to drink?

Discussion

1. Are there many fast food restaurants in your country? Were you surprised by the large number of fast food restaurants in America?

2. Do you like fast food? What are two of your favorite types of fast food?

NOUNS AND NOUN PHRASES—LISTENING

Topic 1: Directions
Exercise A:

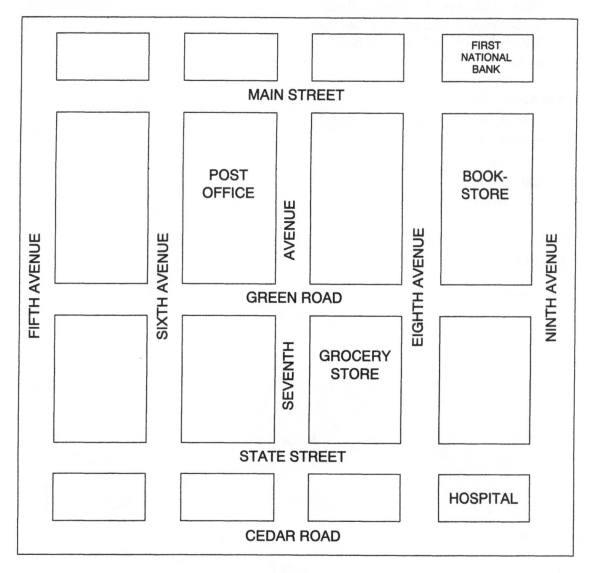

1. First National Bank - Main Street and Ninth Avenue
2. grocery store - corner of State Street and Seventh Avenue
3. hospital - corner of Cedar Road and Eighth Avenue
4. post office - between Green Road and Main Street on Sixth Avenue
5. bookstore - opposite the bank at Main Street and Ninth Avenue

Exercise B:

1. Main Street and Ninth Avenue
2. State Street and Seventh Avenue
3. Cedar Road and Eighth Avenue
4. Green Road and Main Street
5. bank

Exercise C:

1. First National Bank
2. grocery store
3. hospital
4. post office
5. bookstore

Topic 2: Groceries
Exercise A:

Exercise B:

1. biscuits
2. pound
3. bananas
4. pound
5. meat, milk, coffee
6. you

Exercise C:

1. T
2. F
3. T
4. F
5. T

Topic 3: Lost and Found

Exercise A:

gloves
keys
scarf

Exercise B:

1. F
2. F
3. T
4. F
5. T
6. T

Exercise C:

1. Ed's notebook
2. Maggie's wallet
3. Charles' (or Charles's) keys
4. Connie's scarf
5. Ann's fries
6. Jane's salad

Topic 4: Restaurant

Exercise A:

1. T
2. F
3. F
4. F
5. T
6. T

Exercise B:

l. May I take your order please?
2. I'd like a double cheeseburger, large fries, and a salad.
3. What do you have?
4. We have blue cheese, Italian, ranch, and French.
5. I'll have blue cheese.
6. What would you like to drink?

ACTIVITIES

Activity 1: Tourism

Vocabulary

assignment—a job or task

editor—a person in charge of writers or reporters

exported—sold to another country

tourists—people who go sight-seeing to another state or country

> You are a staff member of Sunshine Book Corporation in New York City. Your job is writing books that will give important information to tourists in your city or state in America and make their visit easier. Your latest assignment is to write a short book for foreign visitors. Your editor wants you to base this on your own experiences when you first came to this country.

NOTE: Students should actually produce a small travel guide at the end of the discussions and activities.

A. What are 10 famous places in your city that a person should visit? The first one has been done as an example for you using New York City as the city.

1. Central Park _____

2. _____

3. _____

4. _____

5. _____

6. _____

7. _____

8. _____

9. _____

10. _____

B. Write the name and address of the following places in your city. (If you do not know the address or phone number, call the Chamber of Commerce or check your telephone directory.)

1. Tourist information

    Name: _____

    Address: _____

    Phone: _____

2. Restaurant (Pick two of your favorites.)

    a. Name: _____

        Address: _____

        Phone: _____

    b. Name: _____

        Address: _____

        Phone: _____

3.　Hotel (Pick two of the cheaper ones.)

    a.　Name: _____

       Address: _____

       Phone : _____

    b.　Name: _____

       Address: _____

       Phone: _____

4.　Taxi

   Name: _____

   Address: _____

   Phone: _____

5.　Bank

   Name: _____

   Address: _____

   Phone: _____

6.　Pharmacy

   Name: _____

   Address: _____

   Phone: _____

7. Stores or shopping malls (Pick two of your favorites.)

    a.   Name: _____

          Address: _____

          Phone: _____

    b.   Name: _____

          Address: _____

          Phone: _____

8. Police station

   Name: _____

   Address: _____

   Phone: _____

9. Hospital

   Name: _____

   Address: _____

   Phone: _____

10. Grocery Store

   Name: _____

   Address: _____

   Phone: _____

C. List 20 words a visitor needs to know. The first one has been done as an example for you.

1. subway _____

2. _____

3. _____

4. _____

5. _____

6. _____

7. _____

8. _____

9. _____

10. _____

11. _____

12. _____

13. _____

14. _____

15. _____

16. _____

17. _____

18. _____

19. _____

20. _____

D. List 10 things that a tourist can do in your city or state. (Each answer must include a noun.) The first one has been done as an example for you.

1. Go to see a play. _____

2. _____

3. _____

4. _____

5. _____

6. _____

7. _____

8. _____

9. _____

10. _____

E. List 10 different American foods or drinks a foreigner should try while in America. (Think of your favorites.) The first one has been done as an example for you.

1. pizza _____

2. _____

3. _____

4. _____

5. _____

6. _____

7. _____

8. _____

9. _____

10. _____

F. What are five important things to know about America or Americans? The first one has been done as an example for you.

1.   You should leave a 15 percent tip in most restaurants. (Fast-food restaurants

     are not included.)
     _____

2.   _____

     _____

3.   _____

     _____

4.   _____

     _____

5.   _____

     _____

Discussion:

1.   What do you think of America and Americans? Explain.

2.   Is being in America difficult for you? Explain.

3.   What is one major difference between Americans and people from your country? Explain.

Activity 2: Native Country

Vocabulary

import—something that is bought from another country (Example, gold is imported from South Africa.)

export —something that is sold to another country (Example, cars are exported to Canada.)

Learning about new countries is important, so you and your partner (from a different country) have decided to exchange information and report to the other students. (You should bring in postcards, pictures, travel brochures, etc., of your country; you can obtain such materials as a group on a class trip to a travel agency.)

After getting enough information, you should report to the class on your partner's country.

A. What are four of the most beautiful cities in your country? Explain why you think these cities are beautiful.

1. City: _____

   Reason: _____

   _____

2. City: _____

   Reason: _____

   _____

3. City: _____

   Reason: _____

   _____

4. City: _____

   Reason: _____

B. Where are four popular places to relax and a type of activity that takes place there?

1. Place: _____

    Activity: _____

    _____

2. Place: _____

    Activity: _____

    _____

3. Place: _____

    Activity: _____

    _____

4. Place: _____

    Activity: _____

    _____

C. What are five popular types of food in your country? Describe how one of them is made.

1. _____

2. _____

3. _____

4. _____

5. _____

    _____

    _____

D. What are two types of popular music? Name two popular singers. (Bring in a compact disc (CD) or a cassette tape as an example.)

Music

1. _____

2. _____

Singers

1. _____

2. _____

E. What are three things that are exported from your country? The first one has been done as an example for you.

1. gold _____

2. _____

3. _____

F. What are three of your favorite things about your country? Explain why you like them.

1. _____

   Reason: _____

   _____

2. _____

   Reason: _____

   _____

3. _____

Reason: _____

_____

G. What are three of your least favorite things about your country? Explain why you dislike them.

1. _____

Reason: _____

_____

2. _____

Reason: _____

_____

3. _____

Reason: _____

_____

H. What are three popular types of transportation that people use in your country?

1. _____

2. _____

3. _____

I. Name five famous places (buildings, landmarks, etc.) in your country. Explain why they are famous.

1. Place: _____

Reason: _____

_____

2. Place: _____

    Reason: _____

    _____

3. Place: _____

    Reason: _____

    _____

4. Place: _____

    Reason: _____

    _____

5. Place: _____

    Reason: _____

    _____

J. Are items less or more expensive in America than in your native country? Give some examples comparing prices.

	Your Country	America
1.	gallon of gasoline: _____	$ _____
2.	_____	_____
3.	_____	_____
4.	_____	_____
5.	_____	_____
6.	_____	_____

K. Name two things or people you miss the most from your country. Explain your choices.

1. Thing or person: _____

   Reason: _____

   _____

2. Thing or person: _____

   Reason: _____

   _____

Discussion

1. Of the countries you have heard about, which one would you most like to visit? Why?

2. Describe the education system in your country. Compare it to America's education system. Which one do you prefer? Why?

REVIEW

Key Points

1. A noun names a person, a place, a thing, or an animal.

2. Know the difference between a common noun and a proper noun.

3. Know the difference between a countable and a noncountable noun.

4. Know the ways noun plurals are formed.

5. A singular noun is made possessive by adding an apostrophe and an "s."

6. A plural noun is made possessive by adding an apostrophe after the "s."

7. A pronoun takes the place of a noun.

8. The word the pronoun refers back to is called an antecedent.

9. The antecedent may be a noun or another pronoun.

10. A pronoun can be used as the subject of the sentence, or as the object of a verb or a preposition, or to show ownership (possession).

EXERCISE A: Label the following nouns as being a common noun or a proper noun by writing common noun (CN) or (PN) in the blank provided. The first one has been done as an example for you.

_**CN**_   1. pizza

_____   2. Washington, D.C.

_____   3. December

_____   4. river

_____   5. bottle

_____   6. Friday

_____   7. computer

_____   8. Mississippi River

EXERCISE B: Make the following singular nouns plural. The first one has been done as an example for you.

Singular	Plural
1. child	children
2. doctor	_____
3. lady	_____
4. box	_____
5. shelf	_____
6. airplane	_____
7. boat	_____
8. woman	_____

EXERCISE C: Rewrite the following sentences to show possession. The first one has been done as an example for you.

1. James car was stolen.

   James' (or James's) car was stolen. _____

2. Susan mail arrived before lunch.

   _____

3. The restaurant is owned by Bob Cromer sister.

   _____

4. A nursing assistant job is difficult.

   _____

5. The dog bark is very loud.

   _____

6. The car brakelights did not work.

_____

7. Jorge job starts at 5:00 in the morning.

_____

8. The house is owned by Matuku sister.

_____

EXERCISE D: Underline the prepositional phrases in the following sentences. The first one has been done as an example for you.

1. The brown rabbit ran <u>across the yard</u>.

2. A new house was being built on Hay Street.

3. I live in an apartment on Wise Street.

4. Vickie celebrated her birthday in England this year.

5. We own a house at the lake.

6. Hans returned to Denmark for his mother's birthday.

7. Tom lives in a house by the new mall.

8. They live beside the high school.

EXERCISE E: Underline the pronoun(s) in the following sentences. The first one has been done as an example for you.

1. <u>We</u> cannot go outside because <u>it</u> is raining.

2. I will go to Piedmont Natural Gas to pay my gas bill.

3. My son is napping. Please do not disturb him.

4. Ricardo will never forget the day he passed his driver's test.

5. Susan lost her work keys. She cannot find them.

6. Terri met a friend of hers at the Pioneer Restaurant for lunch.

7. Our house is for sale.

8. Their European history class was canceled.

EXERCISE F: Draw an arrow from the pronoun to its antecedent. The first one has been done as an example for you.

1. Marvin plans to take his college entrance test next Saturday.

2. I will finish writing my research paper this week.

3. Carla has enrolled in her first computer class.

4. We are going to have our family reunion during the Christmas holidays.

5. Where did you get your hair cut?

6. The sales clerk told me that I had 30 days to return the sweater if it did not fit.

7. Sam said he wanted to became a doctor.

8. The Italian restaurant has been sold. It will become a coffee shop.

EXERCISE G: Underline the correct pronoun in the parentheses. The first one has been done as an example for you.

1. Have some cake. (<u>It</u>, Its) is very good.

2. Kevin left the keys in the pocket of (his, him) suit jacket.

3. Tom and Jane invited three friends to dinner at (their, theirs) house last Saturday night.

4. Harold said (he, him) had been laid off from (him, his) job at Rex Plastics.

5. (Mine, My) new refrigerator will be delivered tomorrow.

6. (We, Our) house is for sale; (we, our) plan to move to Florida.

7. (He, His) said (his, him) company was closing in 30 days.

8. (Their, Theirs) family will travel home to Vietnam this summer.

NOUNS AND NOUN PHRASES—REVIEW

ANSWER KEY

Exercise A:

1.	CN	2.	PN	3.	PN	4.	CN
5.	CN	6.	PN	7.	CN	8.	PN

Exercise B:

1. children
2. doctors
3. ladies
4. boxes
5. shelves
6. airplanes
7. boats
8. women

Exercise C:

1. James' (or James's) car was stolen.
2. Susan's mail arrived before lunch.
3. The restaurant is owned by Bob Cromer's sister.
4. A nursing assistant's job is difficult.
5. The dog's bark is very loud.
6. The car's brakelights did not work.
7. Jorge's job starts at 5:00 in the morning.
8. The house is owned by Matuku's sister.

Exercise D:

1. across the yard
2. on Hay Street
3. in an apartment, on Wise Street
4. in England
5. at the lake
6. to Denmark, for his mother's birthday
7. in a house, by the new mall
8. beside the high school

Exercise E:
1. We, it
2. I, my
3. My, him
4. he, his
5. her, she
6. hers
7. Our
8. Their

Exercise F:

1. Marvin plans to take his college entrance test next Saturday.

2. I will finish writing my research paper this week.

3. Carla has enrolled in her first computer class.

4. We are going to have our family reunion during the Christmas holidays.

5. Where did you get your hair cut?

6. The sales clerk told me that I had 30 days to return the sweater if it did not fit.

7. Sam said he wanted to become a doctor.

8. The Italian restaurant has been sold. It will become a coffee shop.

Exercise G:
1. It
2. his
3. their
4. he, his
5. My
6. Our, we
7. He, his
8. Their

ESL
BEGINNER

CHAPTER 3
Verbs and Verb Phrases

Chapter 3

VERBS AND VERB PHRASES

GRAMMAR

Verbs

Verbs are important to sentences. **Verbs** show action and express time.

Examples:

William walks to the post office.

Walks is the verb. Walks shows action.

William walked to the post office.

Walked is the verb. The "-ed" shows the action happened at a past time.

Verb Phrases

Many times a verb can be more than one word. This is called a **verb phrase**. A verb phrase is made up of a **helping verb** (HV) (also called an auxiliary verb) and a **main verb** (MV).

Some common helping verbs are

am	are	can
could	has	have
is	shall	was
were	will	would

A verb phrase may have one, two, or three helping verbs and a main verb.

Examples:

      HV MV

Sue is going to a meeting in Sweden. (one helping verb)

Is going is the verb phrase. *Is* is the helping verb. *Going* is the main verb.

      HV HV MV

Sue will be going to a meeting in Sweden. (two helping verbs)

Will be going is the verb phrase. *Will* and *be* are the helping verbs. *Going* is the main verb.

      HV   HV   HV MV

Sue must have been going to a meeting in Sweden. (three helping verbs) *Must have been going* is the verb phrase. *Must, have,* and *been* are the helping verbs. *Going* is the main verb.

Contractions

The word "not" may be combined with the following helping verbs to form a **contraction**.

Examples:

are + not = aren't	can + not = can't
could + not = couldn't	did + not = didn't
does + not = doesn't	has + not = hasn't
have + not = haven't	is + not = isn't
should + not = shouldn't	was + not = wasn't
will + not = won't	would + not = wouldn't

A contraction expresses a negative. The apostrophe shows that the "o" in "not" has been dropped.

Example:

Carlos did not go to work today because he was sick.

Carlos didn't go to work because he was sick.

Didn't is the contraction for *did not*. The contraction expresses a negative: Carlos is not going to work today.

EXERCISE A: Underline the verb in the following sentences. The first one has been done as an example for you.

1.   Computer skills <u>are</u> important.

2.   Workers arrive at 7:00 in the morning.

3.   Tim works at an art store.

4.   My secretary types 45 words per minute.

5.   Jung's supervisor meets with employees every Monday morning.

6.   The health club plans to add an outdoor track.

EXERCISE B: Underline the verb phrase in the following sentences. Write HV over the helping verb and MV over the main verb. The first one has been done as an example for you.

                  HV MV

1.   Workers <u>can make</u> four tables an hour.

2.   The company president must be going to the meeting.

3.   Employees may take two hours off each month to help at their children's school.

4.   Each salesman will have been traveling for two days.

5.   The company cafeteria will be serving Italian food on Friday.

6.   New employees must attend an insurance benefits meeting at 3:30 this afternoon.

EXERCISE C: Rewrite the following sentences, changing the helping verb + not to a contraction. The first has been done as an example for you.

1. He has not talked to his boss.

    He hasn't talked to his boss.
    _____

2. Helen cannot work until 9:00 at night.

    _____

3. I will not accept your job offer.

    _____

4. Tom does not speak Russian.

    _____

5. The employees have not been wearing their safety glasses.

    _____

6. The workman could not get into the building.

    _____

EXERCISE D: Write six sentences about your workday. Identify the verb or verb phrase in each sentence. The first one has been done as an example for you.

    V
1. I get to work at 5:00 in the morning. _____

2. _____

3. _____

4. _____

5. _____

6. _____

Linking Verbs

Linking verbs are verbs that do not show action. They link the subject to a descriptive word or words. These verbs are also called **state-of-being verbs** because they tell something more about the subject, such as how the person (or thing) feels, looks, or acts.

Some common linking verbs are

appear	look
seem	smell
become	feel

Examples:

The worker looks sick.

Looks is the linking verb. It describes the worker's appearance.

The road seems bumpy.

Seems is the linking verb. It describes the way the road feels.

The verb *to be* is a linking verb. Its forms are:

	Singular	**Plural**
First person:	I *am* late for work.	We *are late* for work.
Second person:	You *are* late for work.	You *are* late for work.
Third person:	He, She, It *is* late for work.	They *are* late for work.

Examples:

He is happy to get more pay.

Juan is happy to get more pay.

He and *Juan* use *is* (the third person singular form of to be).

EXERCISE E: Underline the linking verb in the following sentences. The first one has been done as an example for you.

1.   The food <u>smells</u> good.

2.   The building looks new.

3.   Jim became vice president in 1989.

4.   Our workers appear happy.

5.   Mr. Smith seems tired.

6.   I smell smoke in the kitchen!

EXERCISE F: Practice using the verb "to be" by completing the following sentences. The first one has been done as an example for you.

1.   I <u>am</u> happy to meet you.

2.   The secretary _____ quickly typing the report.

3.   The managers _____ in a meeting.

4.   The company _____ happy moving into a new building.

5.   I _____ glad to get a new job.

6.   The order _____ wrong.

See Appendix E for more information.

Subject-Verb Agreement

The subject must agree with the verb. A singular subject takes a singular verb. A plural subject takes a plural verb.

Examples:

	Singular	**Plural**
First person:	I *work.*	We *work.*
Second person:	You *work.*	You *work.*
Third person:	He, She, It *works.*	They *work.*

NOTE: In the third person singular, the verb must end in "-s".

Examples:

He *works* in a factory.

Tom *works* in a factory.

He and *Tom* are third person singular. The verb *work* must have an "-s" added to it.

The following sentence patterns require special attention to agreement:

Subject + Prepositional Phrase + Verb

The subject may be followed by a prepositional phrase. The prepositional phrase is made up of the preposition and its object (a noun). Some common prepositions are *to, an, in, about, around,* and *from.* The subject must agree with the verb, not the object of the preposition.

Example:

    S   Prep. Phrase   V
The employees on the assembly line work eight hours a day.

The verb is *work.* It must agree with the subject *employees* (plural). *On the assembly line* is the prepositional phrase. *On* is a preposition. *Assembly line* is the object of the preposition.

Indefinite Pronoun + Singular Verb Ending in "-s"

This sentence pattern uses the indefinite pronouns—*each, either, everybody, everyone, somebody,* and *someone.*

The verb must end in "-s".

Examples:

Each employee *wears* safety gloves.

Each is an indefinite pronoun. The verb is *wears*.

Here, There + Verb + Subject

In this sentence pattern, the subject follows the verb.

    V   S
Here are the new uniforms.

    V   S
There is the fire exit.

Where, When, How, What + Verb + Subject

In this sentence pattern, the subject comes after the verb.

Example:

    V   S
Where is the kit?

    V   S
When is the company picnic?

Subject+ Verb + Noun + Who + Verb

who

which

that

Who, *which*, and *that* are relative pronouns. They begin a relative clause. A relative clause tells more information about the noun that comes before it.

Examples:

I work for Mr. Syong, who is a good boss.

Who is a good boss is a relative clause. *Who* is the relative pronoun. The verb in the clause is *is*. *Is* agrees with *Mr. Syong*.

EXERCISE G: Write S over the subject in the following sentences. Underline the correct form of the verb in parentheses. The first one has been done as an example for you.

                      S
1. The new secretary (begin, <u>begins</u>) work tomorrow.

2. James and Frank (writes, write) speeches for the company president.

3. The workman (replace, replaces) the old copy machines.

4. New employees (earn, earns) one hour of personal leave time each month.

5. The computer printer (breaks, break) once a week.

6. The company (plans, plan) to lay off 100 employees.

EXERCISE H: Underline the correct form of the verb in parentheses. The first one has been done as an example for you.

1. The paper in the copier (<u>needs</u>, need) to be replaced.

2. The office (is, are) open.

3. Here (is, are) the new employee benefits booklet.

4. How many people (works, work) for Pica International?

5.   There (is, are) a new salesman in the marketing department.

6.   The conference room in building A (have, has) no windows.

See Appendix F for more information.

Verb Tense

A verb changes form to show when an action happens. This is known as **tense**. Tense expresses time.

Below is a list of verb forms and their definitions:

Simple form—a verb with no ending (such as "-s", "-ed", or "-ing")

Example:

I go to work at 7:00 in the morning.

Go is the simple form of the verb.

Past participle—a form of the past tense that may be combined with a helping verb

Example:

I have gone to buy pens and pencils.

Gone is the past participle of the verb *go*. In this sentence, *gone* is used with the helping verb *have*.

Present participle – "ing" added to the simple form of the verb. The present participle is used with a helping verb.

Example:

I am going to the grocery store after work.

Going ends in "-ing". It is the present participle of the verb *go*. In this sentence, *going* is used with the helping verb *am*.

Infinitive—"to" + the simple form of the verb, such as "to be" and "to work."

I go to work at 7:00 in the morning. *To work* is the infinitive.

Seven verb tenses will be presented in this chapter.

Present Tense

The **present tense** shows that an action is happening now.

Example:

Hong rides the bus to work.

Rides is the verb. *Rides* is in the present tense. It shows that the action is happening now.

NOTE: If the subject of the sentence is a person's name, like Hong; a thing, like an office; or the pronouns he, she, or it, the verb must end in "-s".

Example:

Hong rides the bus to work.

Hong is the subject. *Rides* is the verb. *Rides* ends in "-s" because the subject of the sentence is *Hong*.

Tense Signals

The following words may signal a specific tense:

today (present)

Example:

Sue and Jean work today.

Today shows that the action is happening at the present time.

now (present)

Example:

Sue and Jean have to go to work now.

Now shows that the action is happening at the present time.

yesterday (past)

Example:

Sue and Jean went to work yesterday.

Yesterday shows that the action happened at a past time.

tomorrow (future)

Example:

Sue and Jean will go to work tomorrow.

Tomorrow shows that the action will happen at a future time.

someday (future)

Example:

Sue and Jean will open their own business someday.

Someday shows that the action will happen at a future time.

EXERCISE I: Complete the following sentences by using the present tense form of the verb in parentheses. The first one has been done as an example for you.

1.   John <u>talks</u> (talk) to his supervisor.

2.   The workers in the shipping department _____ (prepare) for inspection.

3.   Health and retirement benefits _____ (be) important to employees.

4.   There _____ (be) a new factory opening in town.

5.   The cost of training new workers _____ (seem) high.

6.   Safety glasses _____ (protect) workers' eyes.

EXERCISE J: Write six sentences using the present tense. The first one has been done as an example for you.

1.   I work at a Mexican restaurant. _____

2.   _____

3.   _____

4.   _____

5.   _____

6.   _____

Past Tense

The **past tense** shows that an action happened at an earlier time.

Example:

Our crew walked to the bus stop.

Walked is the verb. Walked is in the past tense.

The past tense of regular verbs is formed by adding "-ed". *Walk* is a **regular verb**. Its past tense is made by adding "-ed".

Some verbs do not add "-ed" to form the past tense. They are called **irregular verbs**. Irregular verbs change their spelling to form the past tense.

Spelling Tips

TIP A. If the last three letters of the verb are consonant-vowel-consonant (c-v-c), the final consonant is doubled when adding "-ed" or "-ing".

Examples:

> CVC
>
> The truck stopped at the loading dock.

> CVC
>
> The company security officer is stopping at the loading dock.

TIP B. When the verb ends in "-e", the "-e" is dropped when "-ing" is added.

Example:

I am driving to work.

Am driving is the verb. The "-e" has been dropped when the "-ing" is added.

Example:

The artist drew a picture of the new office building.

Drew is the past tense of the irregular verb *draw*.

Main Parts of Commonly Used Irregular Verbs

Present Tense	Past Tense	Past Participle
am/are	was/were	been
arise	arose	arisen
awake	awoke, awaked	awaked, awoken
bear	bore	borne
beat	beat	beaten
become	became	become
begin	began	begun
bend	bent	bent
bind	bound	bound
bite	bit	bitten
bleed	bled	bled
blow	blew	blown
break	broke	broken

Present Tense	Past Tense	Past Participle
bring	brought	brought
build	built	built
burn	burned, burnt	burned, burnt
burst	burst	burst
buy	bought	bought
cast	cast	cast
choose	chose	chosen
cling	clung	clung
come	came	come
creep	crept	crept
deal	dealt	dealt
dig	dug	dug
dive	dived, dove	dived
do	did	done
draw	drew	drawn
dream	dreamed, dreamt	dreamed, dreamt
drink	drank	drunk
drive	drove	driven
eat	ate	eaten
fall	fell	fallen
fight	fought	fought
find	found	found
flee	fled	fled
fling	flung	flung
flow	flowed	flowed
fly	flew	flown
forget	forgot	forgotten
forgive	forgave	forgiven
freeze	froze	frozen
get	got	got, gotten
give	gave	given

Present Tense	Past Tense	Past Participle
go	went	gone
grind	ground	ground
grow	grew	grown
hang (a picture)	hung	hung
hang (a person)	hanged	hung
hear	heard	heard
heat	heated	heated
hide	hid	hidden
hit	hit	hit
hold	held	held
hurt	hurt	hurt
kneel	knelt	knelt
know	knew	known
lay (to place)	laid	laid
lead	led	led
leave	left	left
lend	lent	lent
lie (to rest)	lay	lain
lie (to tell a lie)	lied	lied
light	lighted, lit	lighted, lit
lose	lost	lost
make	made	made
mean	meant	meant
meet	met	met
mistake	mistook	mistaken
pay	paid	paid
prove	proved	proved, proven
put	put	put
read	read	read
rid	rid	rid
ride	rode	ridden

Present Tense	Past Tense	Past Participle
ring	rang	rung
rise	rose	risen
run	ran	run
say	said	said
see	saw	seen
seek	sought	sought
sell	sold	sold
send	sent	sent
set	set	set
sew	sewed	sewn, sewed
shake	shook	shaken
shine	shone	shone
show	showed	shown, showed
shrink	shrank	shrunk
sing	sang	sung
sit	sat	sat
slay	slew	slain
sleep	slept	slept
slide	slid	slid
speak	spoke	spoken
spend	spent	spent
spit	spit, spat	spit, spat
spring	sprang	sprung
steal	stole	stolen
sting	stung	stung
strike	struck	struck
strive	strove	striven
swear	swore	sworn
sweep	swept	swept
swim	swam	swum
swing	swung	swung

Present Tense	Past Tense	Past Participle
take	took	taken
teach	taught	taught
tear	tore	torn
tell	told	told
throw	threw	thrown
thrust	thrust	thrust
wake	woke, waked	woken, waked
wear	wore	worn
weave	wove, weaved	woven, weaved
weep	wept	wept
wind	wound	wound
wring	wrung	wrung
write	wrote	written

EXERCISE K: Complete the following sentences by using the past tense form of the verb in parentheses. See "Main Parts of Commonly Used Irregular Verbs" for a list of irregular past tense verbs (pages 110–114). The first one has been done as an example for you.

1. Tom <u>drove</u> (drive) to Atlanta, Georgia, on business.

2. The employee travel coordinator _____ (be) away from her office.

3. The supervisor _____ (watch) the employee take the crates off the assembly line.

4. The president _____ (speak) to the employees yesterday.

5. The public relations department _____ (write) the sales booklet.

6. New employees _____ (listen) to the supervisor's instructions.

EXERCISE L: Write six sentences using the past tense. The first one has been done as an example for you.

1.   I worked at a Mexican restaurant. _____

2.   _____

3.   _____

4.   _____

5.   _____

6.   _____

Present Perfect Tense

The **present perfect tense** shows that an action occurred in the past and is completed in the present. It is also used to show that an action has just happened. The present perfect tense is made up of the helping verb *has/have* + past participle. The helping verb must agree with the subject. The past participle of regular verbs ends in "-ed". The past participle of irregular verbs changes form. See "Main Parts of Commonly Used Irregular Verbs" for a list of irregular past participles (pages 110–114).

Examples:

Victor has worked at Guilford Plastics for three years.

Has worked is in the present perfect tense. *Has* is the helping verb. *Worked* is the past participle of the regular verb *work*. *Has* agrees with the subject *Victor*. *Has worked* shows Victor began work at Guilford Plastics (three years ago) and works there now.

The men have left for a meeting in Belgium.

Have left is in the present perfect tense. *Have* is the helping verb. *Left* is the past participle of the irregular verb *leave*. *Have* agrees with the subject *men*. *Have left* shows the men have just left for a meeting in Belgium.

EXERCISE M: Complete the following sentences using the present perfect tense. Remember the helping verb must agree with the subject. The first one has been done as an example for you.

1. Conrad Garment Company <u>has stopped</u> (stop) making baseball caps.

2. Jorge _____ (be) self-employed for the past two years.

3. The accountants _____ (complete) their report on the company's sales.

4. Tamicka _____ (leave) her position at Banner Drug Company.

5. Workers _____ (receive) an increase in pay each year.

6. Carlotta _____ (write) the company president's speeches for the past five years.

EXERCISE N: Write six sentences using the present perfect tense. The first one has been done as an example for you.

1. I have worked at a Mexican restaurant for a year. _____

2. _____

3. _____

4. _____

5. _____

6. _____

Past Perfect Tense

The **past perfect tense** shows that one past action happened before another past action. It is made up of the helping verb *had* + past participle.

Example:

After Todd had worked for a year, he asked his boss for more pay.

Had worked is in the past perfect tense. *Had* is the helping verb. Todd's year of work came before he asked for more pay.

EXERCISE O: Complete the following sentences using the past perfect tense. The first one has been done as an example for you.

1. There was a beautiful new office building where the old warehouse <u>had been</u> (be).

2. The company's yearly report said the company _____ (lost) $100,000 last year.

3. Mr. Garcia told the employees that he _____ (sell) the company.

4. I worried about my job because my boss _____ (want) to see my work.

5. Last year I got a new secretary; I _____ (ask) for one for a long time.

6. After Lane's Bowling Alley closed for the night, the people who clean the bowling alley _____ (plan) to polish the bowling lanes.

EXERCISE P: Write six sentences using the past perfect tense. The first one has been done as an example for you.

1. After I had started to work at a Mexican restaurant, I got promoted to manager.

2. _____

3. _____

4. _____

5. _____

6. _____

Present Progressive Tense

The **present progressive tense** shows that an action is happening in the present. It is made up of the helping verbs *am, is, are* + the present participle. The helping verb must agree with the subject.

Example:

Tia is walking to work.

Is walking is in the present progressive tense. *Is* is the helping verb. *Is* agrees with the subject *Tia*. *Is walking* shows that the action is happening now.

EXERCISE Q: Complete the following sentences using the present progressive tense. Remember the helping verb must agree with the subject. The first one has been done as an example for you.

1. Charles and I <u>are getting</u> (get) promoted to assistant manager.

2. The salesman _____ (put) the new shoes on the display rack.

3. The travel agent _____ (arrange) my trip to London, England.

4. Frank _____ (hope) to receive his contract tomorrow.

5. My company _____ (plan) to build a new office building.

6. Roberta and I _____ (learn) to speak Chinese for our upcoming business trip.

EXERCISE R: Write six sentences using the present progressive tense. The first one has been done as an example for you.

1.   Sam is working at a Mexican restaurant. _____

2.   _____

3.   _____

4.   _____

5.   _____

6.   _____

Past Progressive Tense

The **past progressive tense** shows that an action was happening at a specific time in the past. It is made up of the helping verbs *was/were* + the present participle. The subject must agree with the helping verb.

Example:

Betty was working on the computer when her boss telephoned.

Was working is in the past progressive tense. *Was* is the helping verb. *Was* agrees with the subject *Betty*. *Was working* shows when Betty's boss telephoned, Betty was on the computer.

EXERCISE S: Complete the following sentences using the past progressive tense. Remember the helping verb must agree with the subject. The first one has been done as an example for you.

1.   The supervisors <u>were planning</u> (plan) to tell workers about the plant closing.

2.   The machine _____ (shake) when it began to smell of burning rubber.

3. Three new furniture showroom buildings _____ (open) as the International Home Furnishings Market began.

4. I _____ (make) a telephone call to Indonesia.

5. Craig and Louie _____ (drive) trucks when they worked for Vista Chair Company.

6. While Syong worked for Able Electronics, he _____ (put) his younger brothers through college.

EXERCISE T: Write six sentences using the past progressive tense. The first one has been done as an example for you.

1. I was working at the Mexican restaurant when I got accepted to college.

2. _____

3. _____

4. _____

5. _____

6. _____

Future Tense

The **future tense** shows that an action will happen in the future. It is made up of *will* + the simple form of the verb. The helping verb does not change to agree with the subject.

Example:

The company president will retire in June.

Will retire is in the future tense. It shows that the company president's retirement will happen at a future date (in June).

EXERCISE U: Complete the following sentences using the future tense. The first one has been done as an example for you.

1. I <u>will finish</u> (finish) the report tomorrow.

2. All employees _____ (receive) a new insurance card.

3. The repairman _____ (fix) the computer.

4. The old factory _____ (sell) quickly.

5. The Stardust Nightclub _____ (rebuild) after the fire.

6. The meeting _____ (begin) at 6:00 in the evening.

EXERCISE V: Write six sentences using the future tense. The first one has been done as an example for you.

1. I will work at a Mexican restaurant for one year. _____

2. _____

3. _____

4. _____

5. _____

6. _____

Transitive and Intransitive Verbs

A **transitive verb** must have a direct object after it. The direct object tells "who" or "what."

Example:

Emmanuel made a presentation to the board of directors.

Emmanuel is the subject. *Made* is the verb. *Presentation* is the direct object. *Made* is a transitive verb.

An **intransitive verb** does not need a direct object. It can stand alone or complete the meaning of the verb.

Examples:

Emmanuel talked.

Emmanuel is the subject. *Talked* is the verb. *Talked* is intransitive.

Emmanuel talked loudly.

Emmanuel is the subject. *Talked* is the verb. *Talked* is intransitive. *Loudly* completes the meaning of the verb by telling the way Emmanuel talked.

EXERCISE W: Identify the verbs in the following sentences as being transitive (T) or intransitive (I). The first has been done as an example for you.

____T____ 1. The boss asked workers to arrive at 10:00 in the morning.

_____ 2. Tom seems tired after his long business trip.

_____ 3. The benefits manager told employees about the new health insurance plan.

_____ 4. Workers are happy with the new pay increase.

_____ 5. The new building looks huge.

_____ 6. Maria sells jewelry at the department store.

On the following page is a list of verbs. Use the chart as a guide to complete the following exercises.

Present	Past	Past Participle	Present Participle
begin	began	begun	beginning
build	built	built	building
buy	bought	bought	buying
come	came	come	coming
draw	drew	drawn	drawing
drive	drove	driven	driving
find	found	found	finding
leave	left	left	leaving
pay	paid	paid	paying
sell	sold	sold	selling
speak	spoke	spoken	speaking
say	said	said	saying
quit	quit	quit	quitting
wear	wore	worn	wearing
write	wrote	written	writing

EXERCISE X: Complete the sentences with the correct form of the verb. The first one has been done as an example for you.

1. Last week Mr. Carlton <u>wrote</u> (write) a memo to his employees.

2. Tomorrow I _____ (speak) to the employees about plant safety.

3. Because the company has a large order to fill, employees _____ (begin) to come to work earlier.

4. Hung and Jung _____ (sell) their furniture store last year.

5. The company _____ (buy) five acres of land for a new plant.

6. Our employees _____ (wear) uniforms since 1983.

7. When the district manager arrived, all of the employees _____ (left) for the day.

8. At Trite Truck Company, workers _____ (pay) every Friday.

EXERCISE Y: Use the verbs in the chart on page 123 to write six sentences of your own. The first one has been done as an example for you.

1. The company is buying new safety shoes for its employees. _____

2. _____

3. _____

4. _____

5. _____

6. _____

VERBS AND VERB PHRASES—GRAMMAR

ANSWER KEY

Exercise A:
1. are
2. arrive
3. works
4. types
5. meets
6. plans

Exercise B:

    HV MV
1. can make

    HV HV MV
2. must be going

    HV MV
3. may take

    HV HV HV   MV
4. will have been traveling

    HV HV MV
5. will be serving

    HV   MV
6. must attend

Exercise C:
1. He hasn't talked to his boss.
2. Helen can't work until 9:00 at night.
3. I won't accept your job offer.
4. Tom doesn't speak Russian.
5. The employees haven't been wearing their safety glasses.
6. The workman couldn't get into the building.

Exercise D:
Answers will vary.
Here are some examples:

    V
1. I get to work at 5:00 in the morning.

    V
2. I go to lunch at 11:30.

       V
3. My desk is in the office.

       V
4. I like to work in the morning.

       V
5. My boss is very nice.

    V
6. I go home at 4:00 in the afternoon.

Exercise E:

1.	smells	2.	looks	3.	became
4.	appear	5.	seems	6.	smell

Exercise F:

1.	am	2.	is	3.	are
4.	is	5.	am	6.	is

Exercise G:

S
1. secretary, begins
        S
2. James and Frank, write
  S
3. workman, replaces
  S
4. employees, earn
  S
5. printer, breaks
  S
6. company, plans

Exercise H:

1.	needs	2.	is	3.	is
4.	work	5.	is	6.	has

Exercise I:

1.	talks	2.	prepare	3.	are
4.	is	5.	seems	6.	protect

Exercise J:

Answers will vary.
Here are some example sentences:
1. I work at a Mexican restaurant.
2. I am writing in this book.
3. Today is my birthday.
4. I am sitting in a classroom.
5. This class is fun.
6. It is raining.

Exercise K:

1. drove
2. was
3. watched
4. spoke
5. wrote
6. listened

Exercise L:

Answers will vary.
Here are some example sentences:
1. I worked at a Mexican restaurant.
2. I wrote in this book.
3. Yesterday was my birthday.
4. I sat in a classroom.
5. The class was fun.
6. It rained last night.

Exercise M:

1. has stopped
2. has been
3. have completed
4. has left
5. have received
6. has written

Exercise N:

Answers will vary.
Here are some example sentences:
1. I have worked at a Mexican restaurant for a year.
2. I have been writing in this book.
3. I have been celebrating my birthday today.
4. I have been sitting in this classroom.
5. This class has been fun.
6. It has been raining all day.

Exercise O:

1. had been
2. had lost
3. had sold
4. had wanted
5. had asked
6. had planned

Exercise P:

Answers will vary.
Here are some example sentences:
1. After I had started working at a Mexican restaurant, I got promoted to manager.
2. I had written in this book until I filled all the pages.
3. My birthday party had been fun until my uncle got angry.
4. I had been sitting in this classroom until the fire alarm went off.
5. The class had been fun.
6. It had been raining all day.

Exercise Q:

1. are getting
2. are putting
3. is arranging
4. is hoping
5. is planning
6. are learning

Exercise R:

Answers will vary.
Here are some example sentences:
1. Sam is working at a Mexican restaurant.
2. I am helping Sam write in this book.
3. I am celebrating my birthday today.
4. Sam and I are sitting in this classroom.
5. This class is fun.
6. It is raining hard.

Exercise S:

1. were planning
2. was shaking
3. were opening
4. was making
5. were driving
6. was putting

Exercise T:

Answers will vary.
Here are some example sentences:
1. I was working at the Mexican restaurant when I got accepted to college.
2. I was writing in this book until my pen ran dry.
3. Today was my birthday.
4. I was sitting in the classroom when the fire alarm went off.
5. This class was fun until the test began.
6. It was raining when I went home.

Exercise U:

1. will finish
2. will receive
3. will fix
4. will sell
5. will rebuild
6. will begin

Exercise V:

Answers will vary.
Here are some example sentences:
1. I will work at a Mexican restaurant for one year.
2. I will write in this book.
3. It will be my birthday tomorrow.
4. I will sit in this classroom until 1:00.
5. This class will be fun.
6. It will rain tonight.

Exercise W:

1. T	2. I	3. T
4. I	5. I	6. T

Exercise X:

1. wrote	2. will speak	3. have begun
4. sold	5. bought	6. have worn
7. had left	8. are paid	

Exercise Y:

Answers will vary.

Here are some example sentences:

1. The company is buying new safety shoes for its employees.
2. I quit my job yesterday.
3. I should have worn my blue dress.
4. I found my lost cat.
5. I began reading this book yesterday.
6. I will be speaking my lines in the play at tonight's performance.

VISUALIZING PICTURES

Children's Playground

The groundskeeper cuts the bush.

1.	hedge	4.	wheelbarrow	7.	flower
2.	clippers	5.	bush	8.	lawnmower
3.	rake	6.	tree		

EXERCISE: Look at the picture and the labeled items carefully. Write a sentence about the picture using each of the verbs below. The first one has been done as an example for you.

1. look

   The flowers look beautiful.

2. play

3. sits

4. uses

5. bloom

House (under construction)

The carpenter hammers the nail into the wooden beam.

EXERCISE: Look at the picture carefully. Write a sentence about the picture using each of the verbs below. The first one has been done as an example for you.

1. frame

   The wooden beams frame the house.

2. hold

3. hit

4. protect

5. hang

Trucking

The truck driver calls for directions.

1. truck	3. windshield	5. door
2. cab	4. tire	6. antenna

EXERCISE: Look at the picture and the labeled items carefully. Write a sentence about the picture using each of the verbs below. The first one has been done as an example for you.

1. open

   The cab door opens.
   _____

2. look

   _____

3. hold

   _____

4. contain

   _____

5. carry

   _____

Farm

The farmer stands beside his tractor.

1. corn
2. barn
3. tractor
4. cow
5. chicken
6. horse
7. pig

EXERCISE: Look at the picture and the labeled items carefully. Write a sentence about what you see in the picture using each of the verbs below. The first one has been done as an example for you.

1. stand

    The crops stand tall.

2. give

3. eat

4. sow

5. plow

Car Repair Garage

The mechanic fixes the car.

1. car
2. hood
3. tire

4. hubcap
5. wrench
6. screwdriver

7. pliers
8. flashlight

EXERCISE: Look at the picture and the labeled items carefully. Write a sentence about the picture using each of the verbs below. The first one has been done as an example for you.

1. repair

    The mechanic repairs both domestic and foreign cars.

2. hang

3. loosen

4. remove

5. shine

House Fire

The firefighter sprays water to stop the fire.

EXERCISE: Look at the picture carefully. Write a sentence using each of the verbs below. The first one has been done as an example for you.

1. save

    The firefighters save people's lives.
    _____

2. spray

    _____

3. protect

    _____

4. cover

    _____

5. fill

    _____

VERBS AND VERB PHRASES—VISUALIZING VERBS

ANSWER KEY

Children's Playground
Exercise:

Answers will vary.
Here are some examples:
1. The flowers look beautiful.
2. The children play on the swing set.
3. The woman sits on the blanket.
4. The gardener uses the clippers.
5. The flowers bloom in the spring.

House (under construction)
Exercise:

Answers will vary.
Here are some examples:
1. The wooden beams frame the house.
2. The bag holds the carpenter's tools.
3. The hammer hits the nail.
4. The glasses protect the carpenter's eyes.
5. The carpenter's tools hang from her belt.

Trucking

Exercise:

Answers will vary.
Here are some examples:
1. The cab door opens.
2. The man looked at the map.
3. The man holds the phone.
4. The box contains a chair.
5. The truck carries furniture.

Farm

Exercise:

Answers will vary.
Here are some examples:
1. The crops stand tall.
2. The farmer gives corn to the animals to eat.
3. The pig eats corn.
4. The farmer sows seeds to grow corn.
5. The farmer plows his fields.

Car Repair Garage

Exercise:

Answers will vary.
Here are some examples:
1. The mechanic repairs both domestic and foreign cars.
2. Hubcaps hang from the wall.
3. The mechanic uses a wrench to loosen nuts.
4. The hood of the car must be open to remove the air filter.
5. Waxing a car will make it shine.

House Fire

Exercise:

Answers will vary.
Here are some examples:
1. The firefighters save people's lives.
2. The hose is used to spray water onto the fire.
3. The firefighters' helmets protect their heads.
4. The coats cover the firefighters' clothes.
5. The firefighters use water from the hydrant to fill the hose.

READING

Topic 1: Business Hotel

Vocabulary

business traveler—a person who travels as part of his or her job

duplicate—the task done by a copy machine

e-mail— a letter sent by computer

fax—a letter sent over telephone lines

fitness center—a place for a person to exercise

hookup—a special electrical outlet for computers

laptop computer—a small computer that can be taken anywhere

meeting room—a place where discussions about business subjects are held

return—come back

secretary—a person who helps a businessperson with typing, making copies, and filing

security—safety

security guard—a person who is trained in law enforcement (A security guard who works at a hotel makes sure hotel guests are safe.)

serve—to help someone

service—something special offered by a hotel, such as free local calls

Hotels and the Business Traveler

Today, there are many hotels that serve the business traveler. These hotels offer a wide variety of services to make the business traveler feel at home while he or she is away.

Hotels that serve the business traveler have large guest rooms. Each room contains a bed, a desk, a telephone, free coffee, a clock, and a special electrical outlet for computer hookup.

According to Maria Perez, who travels a lot on business, "I like hotels that give you free local telephone calls, a clock, and a big desk in the room. I like a desk big enough for my laptop computer and all my paperwork. Having a special electrical outlet helps too. It means I can plug in my laptop computer and work. Plus, I can send and receive e-mail. This helps me keep in touch with my office. With the alarm clock in the room, I don't have to call the front desk for a wake-up call every morning."

Hotels that serve the business traveler also provide business services to their guests. Guests can use a fax machine. There are meeting rooms. Also, there is a secretary who types letters and reports and duplicates materials for meetings.

Ms. Perez said, "The hotels where I stay should have good lighting in the meeting rooms. I also want the hotel to have a staff person who makes sure I have all the equipment I need, like a blackboard or VCR that works."

Another service offered by these hotels is a fitness center. Max Miller, a front desk clerk at a local hotel that specializes in the business traveler, said, "Our hotel has found that guests want a place to exercise after a long day of work. Our fitness center has a pool and exercise equipment like weights, exercise bikes, and a stair climber. Our guests love it."

Mr. Miller said that security is another concern for business travelers. "We want our guests to feel safe. We have card key entry to our guest rooms. After each guest leaves, the card key security code is changed. We also have a security guard in the lobby 24 hours a day."

Many times the hotels that serve the business traveler offer free transportation to and from the airport. Ms. Perez said that this is important to her since she often does not rent a car.

These hotels want to keep their guests happy. Mr. Miller said, "Good service is important. If a guest asks for an iron and ironing board to press his or her clothes, we will provide one."

Hotels that serve the business traveler want their guests to have a good stay. They want the business traveler to return on his or her next trip to their city.

Comprehensive Questions

EXERCISE A: Answer the following questions about the passage on the lines below.

1. List some services a business traveler might look for in a hotel.

    _____

    _____

    _____

2. What does Maria Perez look for in a hotel?

    _____

    _____

    _____

3. Why is hotel security important?

    _____

    _____

    _____

4. List some of the security measures hotels take.

    _____

    _____

    _____

5. In your opinion, why is good service important?

    _____

    _____

    _____

6. Name some hotels in your area that the business traveler would like.

_____

_____

_____

EXERCISE B: Underline the verb(s) in the following sentences. The first one has been done as an example for you.

1. Many hotels <u>serve</u> the business traveler.

2. Each room contains a bed, a desk, and a telephone.

3. I can send and receive e-mail.

4. I do not have to call the front desk for a wake-up call every morning.

5. Our fitness center has a pool and exercise equipment.

6. These hotels want to keep their guests happy.

Discussion

Tell another student about the times you have stayed in hotels and the services the hotels have provided.

Topic 2: City

Vocabulary

announce—to tell someone

bus terminal—a place for people to get on and off buses

mayor—a person who is in charge of a city or town

remodel—to change how a room looks

residents—people who live in a town or city

vacant—empty

The Magic Block

What can we do with a large, vacant city block in the middle of our downtown? This was the question asked by the residents of High Point, North Carolina. The land, which covered a city block, contained one large building. It used to be a department store. The store closed and moved into the new mall. Owners of this land kept the building empty and rented the parking spaces to downtown businesses for their employee parking.

Since no one really knew what to do with the block, it was called "the magic block." The mayor wanted it used as a bus terminal for the city's transportation system. The residents wanted a park. Then, one day, five businesspeople bought the block.

They announced they would remodel the old department store and turn it into a school to train workers in basic job skills. The businesspeople went on to say that students would receive computer training and a review of math, reading, and English. They also promised to hire a counselor to help the students find jobs.

The residents of High Point were pleased. They felt the training school would benefit everyone.

EXERCISE A: Answer the following questions about the passage on the lines below.

1.   Name some businesses in your downtown which have closed.

_____

_____

_____

2. How has your downtown area changed in the past year? The past five years?

_____

_____

_____

3. In your opinion, does your town have a "magic block"?

_____

_____

_____

4. What types of businesses are located in your downtown?

_____

_____

_____

EXERCISE B: Underline the verb(s) in the following sentences. The first one has been done as an example for you.

1. The store <u>closed</u> and <u>moved</u> into the new mall.

2. The residents wanted a park.

3. Five businesspeople bought the block.

4. They promised to hire a counselor.

5. The residents of High Point were pleased.

6. The training school would benefit everyone.

Discussion

With another student, discuss the differences between the downtown area of the city where you now live and the downtown area of the city where you formerly lived in your native country.

Topic 3: Employees

Vocabulary

CEO—abbreviation for chief executive officer (a person in charge of a company)

close—to bring to an end

community college—a two-year school that trains people for jobs

health insurance—medical services paid for by your company

nurse—a person who helps sick people

orderly—a person who takes sick people from one place to another in a hospital

training—teaching a skill

Factory Closing

Syong was sad. The place where he worked, Artix Blanket Company, was closing. Syong did not know what he would do. He had a family. He wondered how he would feed his children and pay his bills. He wondered when he would find work again.

The CEO said that Syong and the other 750 employees who lost their jobs would receive one full year of pay with prepaid health insurance. This made Syong happy. Then, the CEO told the employees that they could enroll in the local community college, free-of-charge, and receive training in any skill that interested them. Also, Artix would help them find jobs while they attended school.

Syong decided to use the free education to go to a community college and become a nurse. He would see if Artix could help him find a job as an orderly in a hospital. He had turned a bad experience into a positive one that would be good for his family.

EXERCISE A: Answer the following questions about the passage on the lines below.

1.   Explain the CEO's role in the plant closing.

   _____

   _____

   _____

2.   Why is Syong worried?

   _____

   _____

   _____

3.   How has the CEO made the change easier for the employees?

   _____

   _____

   _____

4.   In your opinion, does Syong see happiness despite losing his job?

   _____

   _____

   _____

EXERCISE B: Underline the verb(s) in the following sentences. The first one has been done as an example for you.

1.   Syong <u>was</u> sad.

2.   He had a family.

3.   Atrix would help them find jobs.

4.   They could enroll in the local community college.

5.   Syong decided to use the free education to go to the community college.

6.   He had turned a bad experience into a positive one.

Discussion

Discuss losing a job with another student. Discuss feelings and emotions related to a job loss. Talk about the steps you would take to overcome these feelings.

Topic 4: Business Etiquette

Vocabulary

confidence—a good feeling about oneself

contract—an agreement between two people or businesses

etiquette—manners

firm—strong

Indonesian—a person who lives in Indonesia

order—a request for a product

The Need for Good Business Etiquette

Today companies are requiring employees to take a course on manners in business situations. This is called "business etiquette."

Employees are being taught to greet another businessperson by shaking right hands. The handshake should be firm. Business etiquette professionals say that a firm handshake means confidence.

Business etiquette professionals are working with employees on what to talk about at business dinners. Etiquette professionals say that family matters should not be discussed. For example, at a recent dinner business meeting between an American businessman and an Indonesian businesswoman, the businessman talked about his family problems. The businesswoman told the businessman she would not do business with his company until he learned to place business before family. She went on to say she would take her five-million-dollar order to another company.

Proper business etiquette is important. It can mean more money for a business and better relationships among businessmen and businesswomen.

EXERCISE A: Answer the following questions about the passage on the lines below.

1. Why is good business etiquette important?

   _____

   _____

   _____

2. Why is a firm handshake important?

   _____

   _____

   _____

3. What subject should not be discussed at a business dinner?

   _____

   _____

   _____

4. What is the Indonesian businesswoman's opinion of the American businessman?

_____

_____

_____

EXERCISE B: Underline the verb(s) in the following sentences. The first one has been done as an example for you.

1. Companies <u>are requiring</u> employees to take a course on manners.

2. Employees are being taught to greet another businessperson by shaking right hands.

3. Family matters should not be discussed.

4. The businessman talked about his family problems.

5. Proper business etiquette is important.

6. She would take her five-million-dollar order to another company.

Discussion

With another student, discuss business etiquette situations you have encountered at work. Talk about how you like to dress for work, and how you act differently at work than you do at home.

VERBS AND VERB PHRASES—READING

ANSWER KEY

Topic 1

Exercise A:

1. The services a business traveler might look for in a hotel include a large guest room, free coffee, a desk, a clock in the room, a special electrical outlet in each room for computer hookup, a fax machine, meeting rooms, a secretarial service, good lighting in the meeting rooms, a staff person who looks after the equipment in the meeting rooms, a fitness center, good security, free local calls, free airport transportation, and an iron and ironing board.

2. Maria Perez looks for free local calls, a clock, a big desk, a special electrical outlet for her computer hookup, good lighting in meeting rooms, a staff person to look after the meeting room equipment, and free airport transportation.

3. Hotel security is important to keep guests safe.

4. Security measures include having the card key access code to a room changed after a guest leaves and a security guard in the lobby 24 hours a day.

5. Answers will vary.

6. Answers will vary.

Exercise B:

1. serve
2. contains
3. can send, receive
4. do have
5. has
6. want

Topic 2

Exercise A:

1. Answers will vary.
2. Answers will vary.
3. Answers will vary.
4. Answers will vary.

Exercise B:

1. closed, moved
2. wanted
3. bought
4. promised
5. were pleased
6. would benefit

Topic 3
Exercise A:

1. The CEO told the plant employees how they would be affected by the plant's closing.
2. Syong did not know what he would do. He did not know how he would feed his children or pay his bills, and when he would find work again.
3. The CEO has made the change easier for the employees by explaining they would receive one full year of pay with prepaid health insurance, free education at the local community college, and help in finding new jobs.
4. Answers will vary.

Exercise B:

1. was
2. had
3. would help
4. could enroll
5. decided
6. had turned

Topic 4
Exercise A:

1. Good business etiquette can mean more money for a business and better relationships among businessmen and businesswomen.
2. A firm handshake is important because it means confidence.
3. Family matters should not be discussed at a business dinner.
4. The Indonesian businesswoman thinks the American businessman puts his family before his business.

Exercise B

1. are requiring
2. are being taught
3. should be discussed
4. talked
5. is
6. would take

LISTENING

Topic 1: Weber Furniture Company

Listen as your teacher or partner reads the following:

Welcome to Weber Furniture Company! Weber Furniture makes sofas, chairs, and tables. We employ 500 people. Let me take you on a tour of our plant.

We have two buildings. Building A has offices like the president's office and public relations. Building B is the factory. That's where we make our sofas, chairs, and tables. We also have two classrooms for our employees to attend basic skills classes. They can improve their reading, math, and English skills. Because we believe these skills are so important, we have a teacher who works each of our three shifts. Employees can attend classes the first two hours of their shift.

I hope you will want to come to work for us.

The following directory will tell you about each office or department at Weber Furniture Company:

Building A

benefits—helps workers with their insurance questions

conference room—a room where meetings are held (Weber Furniture has two conference rooms)

indoor garden—flowers, plants, and trees grown inside a building

library—has copies of all sales literature as well as business newspapers and magazines

lobby—where people who visit the factory wait to be seen

payroll—gives out paychecks

personnel—hires new workers

president—in charge of a company

public relations—tells people who do not know about the company news about the company, such as names of new employees or new products for sale

receptionist—a person who greets visitors, answers the telephone, and receives incoming faxes

sales and marketing—people who sell the products to customers

secretary—a person who types, files, and makes copies

vice president—helps the president

Building B

accounts payable—handles the company's bills, like its light bill

accounts receivable—handles money from the stores that buy the furniture

classroom—a room where reading, math, and English classes are held (Weber Furniture Company has two classrooms)

company nurse—gives first aid to workers who are hurt

computer lab—a room with computers and software that help students improve their reading, math, and English

employee cafeteria—place where workers eat

finishing room—where furniture finishes, such as oak or pine, are put on furniture

framing—puts furniture together

inspection—makes sure each piece of furniture is put together properly and is safe to use

loading dock—where trucks load furniture

security—protects the employees and the factory

shipping—sends out furniture

upholstery—puts cloth and padding on sofas and chairs

EXERCISE A: Using the above directory, identify the location of the following offices as being in Building A or Building B. The first one has been done as an example for you.

1. president's office   _____Building A_____

2. security   _____

3. company nurse   _____

4. classroom   _____

5. public relations   _____

6. sales and marketing   _____

7. shipping   _____

8. library   _____

9. vice president's office _____

10. inspection   _____

EXERCISE B: Work with a partner to answer the following questions. Use the words read to you by your teacher or partner and the directory.

1. Name the kinds of furniture made by Weber Furniture Company.

2. What does the receptionist do?

3. What office gives you your paycheck?

4. If you want a cup of coffee and a sandwich, where would you go?

5. What office answers your questions about insurance?

6. Where do you go if you cut your finger?

7. Where do you go to see furniture assembled?

8. Where do you go if you want to apply for a job at Weber Furniture Company?

9. Where does the president's next appointment wait to see him?

10. If you see a man walking around the plant with a shotgun, who do you call?

Discussion:

Tell another student about your workplace. Listen as they tell you about their workplace.

Topic 2: Conversation

Vocabulary

award—being recognized for doing something good

professional resume writer—a person who writes resumes for people

resume—tells where a person has worked, education, and skills

Characters

Sue Miller: Professional resume writer

Ricardo Alvarez: Customer

RICARDO: I need someone to update my resume. I want to apply for a job at Weber Furniture Company.

SUE: I can help you. I am a professional resume writer.

RICARDO: That's great.

SUE: Let me ask you a few questions. What's your name?

RICARDO: Ricardo Alvarez.

SUE: Where were you born?

RICARDO: In Mexico.

SUE: Where do you live?

RICARDO: 555 Oak Street, Johnson City, Tennessee 37614

SUE: What is your telephone number?

RICARDO: 745-555-1213.

SUE: Where have you worked?

RICARDO: I worked at Prime Furniture Company from 1991 to 1996.

SUE: What did you do there?

RICARDO: I worked in the shipping department.

SUE: Did you work in Mexico?

RICARDO: Yes. I was a high school math teacher. I taught for ten years.

SUE: What kind of schooling do you have?

RICARDO: I have a high school degree and degrees in education and math from the Mexico City College.

SUE: Have you received any awards?

RICARDO: Let me see. *(pause)* Yes. I was Employee of the Year at Prime Furniture Company in 1995. When I was a teacher, I received Teacher of the Year in 1989.

SUE: I have all the information I need. I'll type it into the computer. It will be ready tomorrow at 3:00 in the afternoon.

RICARDO: How much will it cost?

SUE: Thirty dollars.

RICARDO: I'll pay you now. *(hands her the money)* Thank you.

EXERCISE: Practice reading the conversation with a partner. You may also wish to practice the conversation supplying your own information instead of Ricardo's words. Then answer the following questions.

1. What kinds of information are included in a resume?

_____

_____

_____

2.   Why is it important to include specific places where you have worked?

_____

_____

_____

3.   Why should you include your education?

_____

_____

_____

4.   In your opinion, does Ricardo need to include any more information?

_____

_____

_____

Discussion

Business magazines state that a resume receives attention for only 30 seconds. Why should a person have a well-written resume that looks neat?

VERBS AND VERB PHRASES—LISTENING

ANSWER KEY

Topic 1: Weber Furniture Company
Exercise A:

1. Building A 2. Building B 3. Building B
4. Building B 5. Building A 6. Building A
7. Building B 8. Building A 9. Building A
10. Building B

Exercise B:

1. sofas, chairs, and tables
2. answers the telephone, greets visitors, and receives faxes
3. payroll
4. company cafeteria
5. benefits
6. company nurse
7. framing
8. personnel
9. lobby
10. security

Topic 2: Conversation
Exercise:

Answers will vary.
Here are some example responses:

1. A resume includes your name, address, where you were born, telephone number, work experience, and education. Also, any awards you have received.
2. It is important to include specific places where you have worked because that is the only way employers will know what experience you have in a particular job.
3. You should include your education to show employers what you have been trained to do.
4. Ricardo might want to include any skills he has, like typing or computer programs.

ACTIVITIES

Activity 1: Crossword Puzzles

Puzzle A

Use the list of occupational titles below to complete the crossword puzzle on the next page. Number one across has been done as an example for you. You may work with a classmate to complete the puzzle.

Occupational Titles

carpenter—a person who builds or fixes things made of wood

farmer—a person who raises animals and crops like corn, green beans, potatoes, or tobacco

firefighter—a person who puts out fires, saves the lives of people and animals, and teaches people about fire safety

groundskeeper—a person who mows lawns, plants flowers, and trims bushes

mechanic—a person who fixes cars and trucks

truck driver—a person who drives food, furniture, or gas from one place to another

ACROSS

1. A _____ cuts grass in a park.

2. A _____ builds houses that are made of wood.

3. The _____ saved my cat's life.

4. A _____ makes his or her living growing corn or tobacco.

DOWN

1. The _____ takes chairs from the factory to the store.

2. A _____ can fix your car.

Note: Answers are given on page 177.

Puzzle B

Use the lists of vocabulary words in the Reading section of this chapter to complete the following crossword puzzle. Number one down has been done as an example for you. You may work with a classmate to complete the puzzle.

ACROSS

1. A discussion about a business subject, like hiring a new employee.

2. A person who lives in a town.

3. Empty

4. A person who works in a doctor's office.

DOWN

1. A person who types letters for a company president.

2. A word that means learning a new skill.

3. A person or business with whom a company does business.

Note: Answers are given on page 177.

Activity 2: Writing (select one)

A. You are a sports reporter for a local radio station. Write a play-by-play account of a football, basketball, soccer, or baseball game. Use verbs that show lots of action.

Example:

The Central High School football player dropped the football. It was picked up by the North High School player. The player ran fast and scored a touchdown. The North High School fans cheered loudly.

B. You are a news reporter for a local radio station. Write a description of an event, like a fire, that is happening now. Use verbs that show lots of action. Example: First National Bank is on fire! Flames are coming out of the windows. People are trapped inside the building. I can hear people shouting, "Help!"

Students should share their work with the class.

Instructors may wish to invite a news or sports reporter from a local radio station to discuss what it is like to cover real-life newsmaking events.

C. You have been asked to write a script for an instructional video on how to perform a common everyday task, such as putting on makeup or making a peanut butter sandwich. Students should work in pairs to create the dialogue and to plan the activity.

Vocabulary

demonstrate—to show how something works (for example, in a department store, a woman may demonstrate how to apply makeup)

dialogue—words spoken by actors or actresses in a film

instruction —teaching

script—printed words actors and actresses speak in a film

video—a film for teaching or entertainment purposes

Instructors may wish to invite someone from the school's learning resource center to videotape students performing their demonstration. The video demonstrations may be shown to the class for critiquing and feedback.

Activity 3: Art

Each student should cut out a picture of a person performing a job and place the picture on posterboard. The student should think of verbs that relate to that job and write them around the picture. Instructors should have students share their work with the class. Instructors also may wish to display students' work on a bulletin board.

REVIEW

Key Points

1. Verbs show action and express time.

2. Verb phrases have a helping verb and a main verb.

3. The subject and the verb must agree.

4. Verb tense shows when an action happened.

5. Know the use of the simple form, past participle, and present participle.

6. Know how verb tenses are formed and used (see chart).

Verb Tense Chart

Tense	How Formed	Use	Example
Present	Uses the simple form of the main verb.	Shows an action is happening now.	Jacques speaks two languages.

Verb Tense Chart

Tense	How Formed	Use	Example
Past	Add "-ed" to the main verb (see pages 110–114 for a list of irregular past tense verbs)	Shows an action happened at an earlier time.	Jacques spoke French at the sales luncheon.
Present-Perfect Tense	has/have + past participle (see pages 110–114 for a list of irregular past participles.)	Shows an action happened in the past and is completed in the present, or just occurred	Jacques has spoken Japanese for two years.
Past-Perfect Tense	had + past participle (see pages 110–114 for a list of irregular past participles.)	One past action happened before another action.	Because Jacques had spoken at the sales luncheon, he got a promotion.
Present-Progressive Tense	am/is/are + present participle	Shows an action that is happening in the present.	Jacques is speaking Japanese.
Past-Progressive Tense	was/were + present participle	Shows an action that happened at a specific time in the past.	Jacques was speaking Japanese when he was interrupted.
Future Tense	will/shall + simple form of the main verb	Shows an action that will happen in the future.	Jacques will speak Japanese at his meeting in Japan.

EXERCISE A: Underline the verb(s) in the following sentences. The first one has been done as an example for you.

1. The Radio Building <u>has</u> ten floors.

2. The truck driver received an award for her safe driving.

3. The salesclerks help customers find cellular telephones and pagers.

4. The managers meet every morning for coffee at Rick's Restaurant.

5. Business colleges train secretaries and computer programmers.

6. The store closes at 4:00 in the afternoon.

EXERCISE B: Underline the verb phrase in the following sentences. The first one has been done as an example for you.

1. Road crews <u>must complete</u> the new highway by summer.

2. Mr. Wong was impressed with the job applicant.

3. Each new employee will be taking his or her hearing test today.

4. Smith Construction is hiring carpenters.

5. Mutuku will return from his business trip to Africa Friday.

6. The CEO has asked the company pilot to get the corporate jet ready for takeoff.

EXERCISE C: Underline the correct form of the verb. The first one has been done as an example for you.

1. The Maple Street warehouse (<u>is</u>, are) empty.

2. There (is, are) 500 workers at the plant.

3. Our company (hires, hire) temporary workers from E-Z Staffing.

4. Where (has, have) the janitor gone?

5. Each employee on the assembly line (wear, wears) safety glasses and gloves.

6. Tom, who (takes, take) orders from customers during the lunch hour, is nice.

7. The desk clerks (answers, answer) questions from hotel guests.

8. The road crew flagperson (directs, direct) traffic through the road construction zone.

EXERCISE D: Complete the following exercises using the present tense form of the verb in parentheses. The first one has been done as an example for you.

1. Carlos <u>is</u> (be) an artist for Lander Advertising.

2. I _____ (work) at Bates Bedding.

3. The results of the plant safety inspection _____ (be) good.

4. All employees _____ (get) one hour for lunch.

5. Many companies in North Carolina _____ (give) the Monday after Easter as a holiday.

6. Hotels _____ (offer) many services like providing fax machines and meeting rooms to business travelers.

EXERCISE E: Complete the following sentences using the past tense form of the verb in parentheses. The first one has been done as an example for you.

1. Yesterday I <u>donated</u> (donate) a pint of blood at the company's annual blood drive.

2. I _____ (work) in New York after graduating from college.

3. Jim _____ (buy) an old warehouse at an auction sale.

4. Ivan _____ (earn) a million dollars last year.

5. A consumer _____ (write) a complaint letter to the company president.

6. The employees _____ (see) a video on plant safety.

EXERCISE F: Complete the following sentences using the present perfect tense form of the verb in parentheses. The first one has been done as an example for you.

1. Anthony <u>has completed</u> (complete) a two-year program in accounting.

2. Charles and Edward _____ (buy) Plastic Concepts.

3. The CEO _____ (speak) to the press about the recent layoffs.

4.   For two years, I _____ (wait) for a promotion.

5.   Ivan _____ (handle) customers' complaints for ten years.

6.   Since coming to the United States, I _____ (work) as a janitor.

EXERCISE G: Complete the following sentences using the past perfect tense form of the verb in parentheses. The first one has been done as an example for you.

1.   Susan told her co-workers that she <u>had planned</u> (plan) to change jobs.

2.   The annual report said that the company _____ (lose) ten million dollars in 1994.

3.   Last year I bought an Italian restaurant; I _____ (want) to own one for years.

4.   By the time the training and development manager spoke to us, I _____ (decide) to return to school to get my GED.

5.   Josh _____ (write) the report, but he had forgotten to save a copy on the computer disk.

6.   The employee newsletter said the company picnic _____ (be) a success.

See Appendix G for more information.

EXERCISE H: Complete the following sentences using the present progressive form of the verb in parentheses. The first one has been done as an example for you.

1.   Tina <u>is working</u> (work) at North State Container.

2.   Eloise and I _____ (develop) a business plan for our new flower shop.

3.   The company _____ (get) a new CEO.

4.   The customer service representative _____ (process) our order.

5.   Anton and Vivian _____ (walk) around the office complex during lunch.

6.   We _____ (buy) a new factory in eastern Michigan.

EXERCISE I: Complete the following sentences using the past progressive form of the verb in parentheses. The first one has been done as an example for you.

1.   I <u>was practicing</u> (practice) my speech to give to the management team with Matthew.

2.   We _____ (wonder) if the company made a profit this year.

3.   When the CEO arrived, we _____ (give) our presentation.

4.   The employees _____ (work) when the smoke alarm sounded.

5.   Julie _____ (ride) the subway when her briefcase was stolen.

6.   Leland _____ (sit) at the computer when his wife telephoned.

EXERCISE J: Complete the following sentences using the future tense form of the verb in parentheses. The first one has been done as an example for you.

1.   I <u>will relocate</u> (relocate) to Japan next year.

2.   Victor _____ (get) more pay after six months of being employed with Paper City.

3. Isabella _____ (meet) three new clients tomorrow.

4. New students _____ (take) the entering reading and math tests at Midville Community College on Saturday.

5. I _____ (see) you at the sales meeting tomorrow.

6. The secretary _____ (type) your report tomorrow afternoon.

VERBS AND VERB PHRASES—REVIEW

ANSWER KEY

Exercise A:
1. has
2. received
3. help
4. meet
5. train
6. closes

Exercise B:
1. must complete
2. was impressed
3. will be taking
4. is hiring
5. will return
6. has asked

Exercise C:
1. is
2. are
3. hires
4. has
5. wears
6. takes
7. answer
8. directs

Exercise D:
1. is
2. work
3. are
4. get
5. give
6. offer

Exercise E:
1. donated
2. worked
3. bought
4. earned
5. wrote
6. saw

Exercise F:
1. has completed
2. have bought
3. has spoken
4. have waited
5. has handled
6. have worked

Exercise G:
1. had planned
2. had lost
3. had wanted
4. had decided
5. had written
6. had been

Exercise H:
1. is working
2. are developing
3. is getting
4. is processing
5. are walking
6. are buying

Exercise I:
1. was practicing
2. were wondering
3. were giving
4. were working
5. was riding
6. was sitting

Exercise J:

1. will relocate
2. will get
3. will meet
4. will take
5. will see
6. will type

Activity 1:

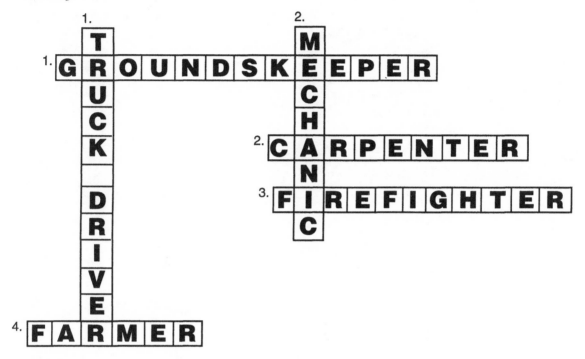

Activity 2:

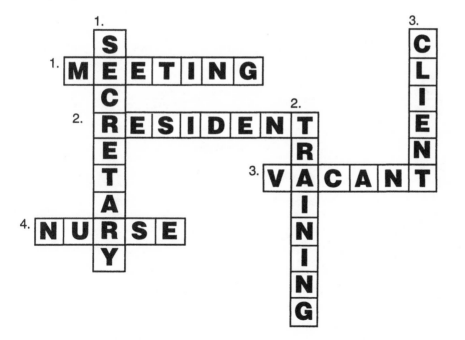

ESL

BEGINNER

CHAPTER 4
Simple Sentences

Chapter 4

SIMPLE SENTENCES

GRAMMAR

Simple Sentence

A **simple sentence** is a group of words that expresses a complete thought.

Example:

Maria works at Carolina Furniture.

Types of Simple Sentences

There are four (4) types of simple sentences.

1. A **declarative sentence** tells something.

   Example:

   The business opened in 1990.

2. An **imperative sentence** tells a person to do something. (An imperative sentence is also known as a **command**. The subject of the sentence is understood to be "you.")

   Example:

   Put on your safety glasses. (*You* put on your safety glasses.)

3. An **interrogative sentence** asks a question.

   Example:

   When will the nurse arrive?

4. An **exclamatory sentence** shows a strong feeling.

    Example:

    Your presentation was wonderful!

Punctuation

A simple sentence begins with a capital letter.

Example:

Workers arrive at 5:00 in the morning.

The word *workers* begins the sentence. The first letter *W* is capitalized.

The simple sentence ends with either a period (.), an exclamation point (!), or a question mark (?).

1. A **period** ends a declarative or imperative sentence.

    Example:

    Twenty people will work at the new factory. (declarative sentence)

    Tell the workers coffee break is over. (imperative sentence)

2. An **exclamation point** ends an exclamatory sentence.

    Example:

    Call the nurse!

3. A **question mark** ends an interrogative sentence.

    Example:

    How many people work at Stamos Industries?

EXERCISE A: Identify each of the following sentences as declarative, imperative, interrogatory, or exclamatory. The first one has been done as an example for you.

1. I work on an assembly line.   _____Declarative_____

2. When will the company shut down?   _____

3. Watch out for falling bricks!   _____

4. That was a great slide show.   _____

5. How long will the test take?   _____

6. My job is very interesting.   _____

EXERCISE B: Rewrite the following word groups by beginning each one with a capital letter and ending with a period, question mark, or exclamation point. The first one has been done as an example for you.

1. when did Sarat begin his job

   When did Sarat begin his job? _____

2. her shift begins at midnight

   _____

3. put on your gloves

   _____

4. the desk clerk helped the guest

   _____

5. what are the hours of the employee health clinic

   _____

Subjects and Verbs

A simple sentence has one subject and one verb. The **subject** (S) tells what the sentence is about. The **verb** (V) shows action.

Example:

Maria works at Carolina Furniture.

Maria is the subject. The sentence is about Maria.

Works is the verb. It tells what Maria does.

Verbs that do not show action are called **linking verbs** (LV). Linking verbs link the subject to a descriptive word or words. Some common linking verbs are:

to be (am, are, is, was, were)	look
appear	seem
become	smell
feel	stay

Example:

The worker seems tired.

Worker is the subject.

Seems is the linking verb.

Tired describes how the worker feels.

Many times a verb may be more than one word. This is called a **verb phrase**. A verb phrase contains a **helping verb** (auxiliary verb) [HV] and a **main verb** [MV]. The **helping verb** (also called an auxiliary verb) helps the main verb to show action. The **main verb** is the final verb in a verb phrase.

Example:

Maria has worked at Carolina Furniture.

Maria is the subject.

Has is the helping verb.

Worked is a form of the verb *work*.

Some common helping verbs are:

am	been	can
could	has	have
must	shall	was
were	will	would

NOTE: The verb "to be" can be used either as a helping verb or a linking verb.

Example:

Maria is going to the Personnel Office.

Maria is the subject.

Is is the helping verb. *Going* is the main verb.

Maria is happy with her new job.

Maria is the subject.

Is is a linking verb. *Happy* describes how Maria feels.

A verb phrase may be made up of one, two, or three helping verbs and a main verb.

Examples:

     HV   MV

Maria *is working* at Carolina Furniture.

       HV   HV   MV

Maria *would have worked* at Carolina Furniture.

       HV   HV   HV   MV

Maria *would have been working* at Carolina Furniture.

In some sentences, the helping verb may come before the subject. This is called an **inverted sentence** and is a question.

Example:

HV   S   MV

Is Maria working at Carolina Furniture?

EXERCISE C: Underline the subject in the following simple sentences. The first one has been done as an example for you.

1.   The <u>foreman</u> has ordered a new forklift.

2.   The secretary will deliver the memos.

3.   The manager hires all new employees.

4.   Applicants for the supervisor's job look impressive.

5.   Plans for the new plant look good.

6.   The chef's new dessert smells delicious.

EXERCISE D: Underline the verb(s) in the following simple sentences. The first one has been done as an example for you.

1.   Workers <u>can wear</u> their old uniforms.

2.   The supervisor will listen to an employee's concerns.

3.   The chef will train his new assistant.

4.   The workers appear angry.

5.   The president's remarks were inspiring.

6.   The weaving machine is broken.

Additional Parts of the Simple Sentence

A **prepositional phrase** is a group of words that tells about another word. Some common prepositions are *at, to, for, from, above,* and *below.*

Example:

Maria works at Carolina Furniture.

Maria is the subject.

Works is the verb.

At Carolina Furniture is the prepositional phrase.

A **direct object** (DO) comes after the verb. The direct object tells "What?" or "Whom?".

Example:

Thomas remembered his boss fondly.

Thomas is the subject.

Remembered is the verb.

His boss is the direct object. The phrase follows the verb *remembered* and tells "Thomas remembered whom?"

An **indirect object** (IO) comes before the direct object. The indirect object tells *to* or *for whom* the action of the verb was done.

Example:

The supervisor promised me a raise.

Supervisor is the subject.

Promised is the verb.

Me is the indirect object and tells to whom the verb *promised* was made.

Raise is the direct object and answers the question "The supervisor promised what?"

A **subject complement** (SC) comes after the linking verb. The subject complement tells something about the subject.

Example:

Mr. Syong is the new manager.

Mr. Syong is the subject.

Is is the linking verb.

New manager is the subject complement and tells about the subject *Mr. Syong*.

Sentence Patterns

Simple sentences follow four patterns. They are:

1.   Subject + Verb

     S   V

     Example: Maria works.

2.   Subject + Verb + Direct Object

     S   V   DO

     Example: Maria read the memo.

3.   Subject + Verb + Indirect Object + Direct Object

     S   V   IO   DO

     Example: Maria read me the memo.

4.   Subject + Linking Verb + Subject Complement

     S LV   SC

     Example: Maria is the new office manager.

EXERCISE E: Identify the subject and verb in each of the following sentences by writing an S over the subject and a V over the verb. The first one has been done as an example for you.

         S   V

1.   Samuel has returned from a meeting in Brazil.

2.   The meeting ended at 12 noon.

3.   The president gave employees a two-week vacation.

4.   Mr. Symthe resigned as CEO of Gibson Toy Company.

5.   Our workday will begin at 7:00 in the morning.

6.   Wolfgang will be working a third shift this week.

EXERCISE F: Identify the sentence pattern used in the following sentences. The patterns are listed below. The first one has been done as an example for you.

A.   Subject + Verb

B.   Subject + Verb + Direct Object

C.   Subject + Verb + Indirect Object + Direct Object

D.   Subject + Linking Verb + Subject Complement

   D   1. My supervisor must have been promoted.

_____ 2. The snowstorm caused us to lose money.

_____ 3. Carol left on her business trip.

_____ 4. Sales increased this month.

_____ 5. My secretary is a good typist.

_____ 6. He repaired the copy machine.

EXERCISE G: Write six sentences about your workday. Identify the subject and verb in each sentence. The first one has been done as an example for you.

         S V

1.   **I work in a factory.** _____

2.   _____

3.   _____

4.   _____

5.   _____

6.   _____

See Appendix H for more information.

Fragments

A **fragment** is a group of words that does not express a complete thought. A fragment lacks a subject, a verb, or both.

Example:

Have bought a puppy.

This word group is a fragment. It is made up of the helping verb *have* + the main verb *bought* and a direct object *puppy*. The word group lacks a subject. Below is the same sentence revised.

Juan and Maria have bought a puppy.

The subject *Juan and Maria* have been added to make the word group into a simple sentence.

The following chart shows some common types of fragments.

Type	Fragment	Sentence
Noun Phrase	The beautiful dog.	The beautiful dog belongs to me.

(See Chapter 2 for an explanation of noun phrases.)

Prepositional Phrase	In the pet shop.	I enjoy going to the pet shop.

(See Chapter 2 for an explanation of prepositional phrases.)

Verb Phrase	Must have been studying.	I must have been studying.

(See Chapter 3 and pages 184 and 185 of this chapter for an explanation of verb phrases.)

Subordinate Clause	When I was twenty years old.	When I was twenty years old, I bought my first car. I bought my first car when I was twenty years old.

NOTE: A subordinate clause is a word group that may confuse the writer. A subordinate clause begins with a subordinating conjunction (*after, although, because, before, if, since, until, when, whenever, while*). A subject and verb follow the subordinating conjunction; however, the word group is not a sentence. It is a fragment. In order for the word group to be a sentence, a sentence must be added before or after the subordinate clause. If the subordinate clause begins a sentence, it must be followed by a comma. If a subordinate clause ends a sentence, no comma is needed.

Examples:

When I was twenty years old, I bought my first car.

This sentence begins with the subordinate clause *When I was twenty years old*.

A comma follows the clause. *I bought my first car* is the sentence. *I* is the subject. *Bought* is the verb.

I bought my first car when I was twenty years old.

This sentence ends with the subordinate clause *when I was twenty years old*.

I bought my first car is the sentence. *I* is the subject. *Bought* is the verb. No comma is needed because the subordinate clause ends a sentence.

EXERCISE H: Identify the following word groups as being a sentence or a fragment by writing S (sentence) or F (fragment) in the blank provided. The first two exercise items have been done as an example for you.

__S__   1. Chan lives in Los Angeles, California.

__F__   2. In the hospital.

_____   3. The community college's ESL class begins at 6:00 in the evening.

_____   4. Because I was sick, I missed two days of work.

_____   5. May be going to the mall.

_____   6. While I was at the bank.

_____   7. Vicki went to the dentist because her tooth hurt.

_____   8. A big boat.

EXERCISE I: Rewrite the following fragments into sentences. The first one has been done as an example for you.

1.   Near the music shop on Oakland Avenue.

   Chu lives near the music shop on Oakland Avenue.
   _____

2.   Going to the beach for a week.

   _____

3.   A small house.

   _____

4.   The big dog on Second Avenue.

   _____

5.   When I was a child.

   _____

Interrogative Sentence

An **interrogative sentence** begins with an interrogative pronoun and ends with a question mark. An interrogative sentence asks a question. The interrogative pronouns are:

what	when
why	where
how	who

Examples:

What are the new safety regulations?

Why must we wear safety shoes?

How did you get to be manager?

When does third shift begin?

Where is the company nurse?

Who is the new quality control manager?

There are three (3) types of questions:

1.   Information Questions

2.   Yes/No Questions

3.   Tag Questions

Information Questions

Information questions ask for a specific response.

Example:

How many sofas are made each day?

Response: Twelve sofas are made each day.

Yes/No Questions

Yes/No questions are answered with a "yes" or "no" response. "Yes" indicates a positive response. "No" indicates a negative response.

Examples:

Question: Do you work?

Response: Yes, I work as a janitor.

Question: Do you work?

Response: No, I don't work.

This type of question often uses a linking verb *(am, is, are, was, were)* in its response.

Example:

Question: Are you a lawyer?

Response: Yes, I am a lawyer.

Am is a linking verb.

Tag Questions

A **tag question** occurs when someone is unsure about the response to a question. A tag is placed at the end.

Example:

You are a truck driver, aren't you?

The first part of the question ("You are a truck driver") is positive (yes) while the second part ("aren't you") is negative (no). A tag question is used to tell if a person is telling the truth. A tag question might be used in a job interview to tell if a person is giving the correct information about himself or herself.

Examples:

Question: You are a truck driver, aren't you?

Response: Yes, I am.

Question: You are a truck driver, aren't you?

Response: No, I'm a dishwasher at a restaurant.

EXERCISE J: Practice using the interrogative pronouns by asking these questions to a classmate and writing down the responses. The instructor may wish to have the students present their responses to the class. The first one has been done for you as an example .

1. How old are you?

   I am 25 years old.
   _____

2. What is your name?

   _____

3. What is your native country?

   _____

4. How long have you lived in the United States?

   _____

5. What do you do for a living?

   _____

6. Where do you work?

   _____

EXERCISE K: Respond to the following information questions by using simple sentences. The first one has been done for you as an example.

1. How many years have you worked as a cook?

   I have worked as a cook for two years.
   _____

2. What is today's date?

    _____

3. Where were you born?

    _____

4. When is your birthday?

    _____

5. What was your first job?

    _____

6. Who is your boss?

    _____

EXERCISE L: Respond to the following questions by writing a "yes" or "no" response. The first one has been done for you as an example.

1. Do you type?

    No, I don't type.
    _____

2. Do you have a green card?

    _____

3. Are you a United States' citizen?

    _____

4. Do you have a driver's license?

    _____

5. Do you work first shift?

_____

6. Are you a resident alien?

_____

EXERCISE M: Practice responding to these tag questions orally with a class-mate. The first one has been done for you as an example.

1. You work for Mac Panel, don't you?

   No, I work for Wang Plastics.

2. You work in a large office building, don't you?

   _____

3. You can get a higher paying job, can't you?

   _____

4. You have to sign in when you get to work, don't you?

   _____

5. You have to wear safety clothing at work, don't you?

   _____

6. You always tell your supervisor if you get hurt on the job, don't you?

   _____

See Appendix I for more information.

SIMPLE SENTENCES—GRAMMAR

ANSWER KEY

Exercise A:

1. Declarative
2. Interrogative
3. Exclamatory
4. Declarative
5. Interrogative
6. Declarative

Exercise B:

1. When did Sarat begin his job?
2. Her shift begins at midnight.
3. Put on your gloves!
4. The desk clerk helped the guest.
5. What are the hours of the employee health clinic?

Exercise C:

1. foreman
2. secretary
3. manager
4. Applicants
5. Plans
6. dessert

Exercise D:

1. can wear
2. will listen
3. will train
4. appear
5. were
6. is

Exercise E:

```
        S       V
```
1. Samuel has returned from a meeting in Brazil.

S   V
2. The meeting ended at 12 noon.

        S   V
3. The president gave employees a two-week vacation.

        S   V
4. Mr. Symthe resigned as CEO of Gibson Toy Company.

        S   V
5. Our workday will begin at 7:00 in the morning.

     S   V
6. Wolfgang will be working a third shift this week.

Exercise F:

1. D	2. C	3. B
4. B	5. D	6. B

Exercise G:

Answers will vary.
Here are some examples:

    S V
1. I work in a factory.

       S V
2. My job is very challenging.

    S V
3. I drive my car to work.

       S   V
4. My co-workers are nice people.

    S V
5. I go to lunch at noon.

    S   V
6. I have worked at my job for two years.

Exercise H:

1. S	2. F	3. S
4. S	5. F	6. F
7. S	8. F	

Exercise I:

Answers will vary.
Here are some examples:
1. Chu lives near the music shop on Oakland Avenue.
2. My family is going to the beach for a week.
3. My uncle lives in a small house.

4. I am scared of the big dog on Second Avenue.
5. My mother gave me piano lessons when I was a child.

Exercise J:

Answers will vary.
Here are some examples:
1. I am 25 years old.
2. My name is Hong Chen.
3. My native country is Taiwan.
4. I have lived in the United States for two years.
5. I am an engineer.
6. I work in an office.

Exercise K:

Answers will vary.
Here are some examples:
1. I have worked as a cook for two years.
2. Today's date is January 28th.
3. I was born in Taipei, Taiwan.
4. My birthday is April 3rd.
5. My first job was as a kitchen helper in a restaurant.
6. My boss is the owner of the restaurant.

Exercise L:

Answers will vary.
Here are some examples:
1. No, I don't type.
2. Yes, I have a green card.
3. No, I am not a United States citizen.
4. Yes, I have a driver's license.
5. Yes, I work first shift.
6. Yes, I am a resident alien.

Exercise M:

Answers will vary.
Here are some examples:
1. No, I work for Wang Plastics.
2. No, I work in a small factory.
3. Yes, I could get a higher paying job.
4. Yes, I have to sign my timecard when I get to work.
5. Yes, I have to wear safety glasses and gloves at work.
6. Yes, I always tell my supervisors when I get hurt on the job.

VISUALIZING PICTURES

Office

The secretary writes in her appointment book.

The subject of the sentence is *secretary*. A secretary is a person who works for someone in a company like the president, vice president, or personnel manager. A secretary should know how to use a computer and a calculator, and how to answer the telephone in a professional, courteous manner. A secretary may also be called an administrative assistant or personal assistant. The verb *writes* means to use pen and paper or to make a record of a meeting or conference times for his or her boss. In this picture, the secretary is writing the times of her boss' meetings and conferences in her appointment book.

EXERCISE: Use the list of possible subjects and verbs below to write your own sentences about what you see in the picture. You may use each word more than once. The first one has been done as an example for you.

Subjects	Verbs
woman	contains
telephone	looks
computer	wears
calculator	lists
appointment book	rings

1. The telephone rings.

2. _____

3. _____

4. _____

5. _____

Restaurant

The waiter takes the customer's order.

1. table	5. spoon	9. menu
2. chair	6. fork	10. painting
3. tablecloth	7. knife	11. pad
4. plate	8. napkin	12. pen

The subject of the sentence is *waiter*. A waiter works in a restaurant. A waiter writes on a pad the food a customer wants and brings the customer the food. The verb *takes* means to get something from another person. In this picture, the waiter is getting an order from the customer.

EXERCISE: Use the list of possible subjects (some are labeled in the picture) and verbs below to write your own sentences about what you see in the picture. You may use each word more than once. The first one has been done as an example for you.

Subjects	Verbs
waiter	taste
menu	takes
tablecloth	eats
plate	serves
men	read
women	covers

1. The men and women are reading the menu. _____

2. _____

3. _____

4. _____

5. _____

Hospital

The nursing assistant uses a thermometer to check the patient's temperature.

The subject of the sentence is *nursing assistant*. A nursing assistant works in a hospital, a nursing home, or a doctor's office. A nursing assistant checks a patient's vital signs—temperature, blood pressure, and pulse. The verb *uses* means to make something act in a certain way. In this picture, the nursing assistant is using the thermometer to check the patient's temperature.

EXERCISE: Use the list of possible subjects and verbs below to write your own sentences about what is happening in the picture. You may use each word more than once. The first one has been done as an example for you.

Subjects	**Verbs**
patient	hangs
thermometer	lies
light	takes
nursing assistant	raises
stethoscope	wear
bed	shines

1. The patient raises the bed by pressing a button on the side rail. _____

2. _____

3. _____

4. _____

5. _____

Clothing Store

The sales clerk shows a dress to a customer.

1. dress
2. coat
3. rack
4. counter
5. cash register
6. size label

The subject of the sentence is *sales clerk*. A sales clerk works in a clothing store, convenience store, or department store. A sales clerk helps people find something like a dress. A sales clerk may also be called a sales associate or sales counselor. The verb *shows* means to point out an object. In this picture, the sales clerk is pointing out a dress to a customer.

EXERCISE: Use the list of possible subjects (some are labeled in the picture) and verbs below to write your own sentences about what is happening in the picture. You may use each word more than once. The first one has been done as an example for you.

Subjects	Verbs
dress	selects
sales clerk	chooses
customer	pays
cash register	hangs
sign	says

1. The customer chooses a dress.

2. _____

3. _____

4. _____

5. _____

Daycare

The preschool teacher reads to the children.

The subject of the sentence is *preschool teacher*. A preschool teacher works in a day-care center. A preschool teacher works with children under the age of five. The verb *reads* means to tell a story. In this picture, the preschool teacher is reading a story out loud to her children.

EXERCISE: Use the list of possible subjects and verbs below to write your own sentences about what you see in the picture. You may use each word more than once. One has been done as an example for you.

Subjects	Verbs
lion	read
children	roars
truck	rolls
shelves	fill
book	sits
teacher	play

1. The lion roars. _____

2. _____

3. _____

4. _____

5. _____

Kitchen

The chef cooks fish.

The subject of the sentence is *chef*. A chef works in the kitchen of a restaurant, a hospital, or a school. The verb *cooks* means to prepare food. In this picture, the chef is preparing fish.

EXERCISE: Use the list of possible subjects and verbs below to create sentences of your own. You may use the same words more than once. The first one has been done as an example for you.

Subjects	Verbs
fish	contains
knife	cuts
oven	bakes
pot	cooks
counter	looks

1. The knife is used to cut fish. _____

2. _____

3. _____

4. _____

5. _____

SIMPLE SENTENCES—VISUALIZING PICTURES

ANSWER KEY

Exercise: Office

Answers will vary.

Here are some examples:

1. The telephone rings.
2. The woman wears a jacket.
3. The appointment book contains notes on meetings.
4. The woman lists dates in her appointment book.
5. The woman looks busy.

Exercise: Restaurant

Answers will vary.

Here are some examples:

1. The men and women are reading the menu.
2. The tablecloth covers the table.
3. The waiter takes their order.
4. The waiter will serve their food.
5. The man asks the waiter how the food tastes.

Exercise: Hospital

Answers will vary.

Here are some examples:

1. The patient raises the bed by pressing a button on the side rail.
2. The nursing assistant takes the patient's temperature with a thermometer.
3. The nursing assistant wears a stethoscope.
4. A light hangs over the bed.
5. The patient lies in the bed.

Exercise: Clothing Store

Answers will vary.

Here are some examples:

1. The customer chooses a dress.
2. The dresses hang from the racks.
3. The sales clerk selects dresses for the customer to try on.
4. The customer pays for the dress at the cash register.
5. The sign says what sizes the dresses are.

Exercise: Daycare

Answers will vary.

Here are some examples:

1. The lion roars.
2. The children sit in front of the teacher.
3. The shelves are filled with toys.
4. The teacher reads to the children.
5. The truck rolls on big wheels.

Exercise: Kitchen

Answers will vary.

Here are some examples:

1. The knife is used to cut fish.
2. The chef cooks vegetables in the pot.
3. The oven is used to bake pies.
4. The fish looks cooked.
5. The chef cuts the fish on the counter.

READING

Topic 1: Finding a Job

Vocabulary

advertisement—a promotional notice in print, on the Internet, over the airwaves or in cablecasting

Career Development Office—an on-campus office where businesses can list job openings

college—a school that a student attends after graduating from high school

employment agency—a type of business that finds a person a job

Employment Security Commission—a state-funded business that will help a person find a job

resources—places to go for help

server—a person who serves food and drink

tailor—a person who makes or alters clothes

temporary employment agency—a type of business that finds a person a job for a few days or weeks

workplace—a place where people work

Today there are many resources available to a person looking for a job. Newspapers contain advertisements of job openings. The jobs are arranged in order of job title, such as "mechanic," "nurse," "server," and "tailor." Employment agencies can also help a person find a job. The Employment Security Commission can help a person find a job in his or her city. There are temporary employment agencies that can find a person a job for a few days or weeks. A person's friends can also help him or her find a job. Many times a friend will let you know if there is an opening at his or her workplace. Finally, many colleges have a Career Development Office. Local employers will notify this office of job openings, and the college will provide the workers. A person looking for a job should use all resources available to him or her.

EXERCISE A: Answer the following questions on the lines below.

1. In your opinion, is finding a job today easy or difficult?

    _____

    _____

    _____

2. List some agencies in your area that can help a person find a job.

    _____

    _____

    _____

3. How can your school help you find a job?

    _____

    _____

    _____

4. Based upon your experience, what is the best way to find a job?

    _____

    _____

    _____

EXERCISE B: Identify the following word groups as being a sentence or a fragment by writing S (sentence) or F (fragment) in the blank provided. The first one has been done as an example for you.

____S____ 1. There are many resources available to a person trying to find a job.

_____ 2. Job titles, such as mechanic, nurse, waitress, and seamstress.

_____ 3. The Employment Security Commission can help a person find a job in his or her city.

_____ 4. That a person can find a job for a few days or weeks.

_____ 5. Resources available to him or her.

_____ 6. Many colleges have a Career Development Office.

Discussion

Have students discuss their job search experiences. The teacher might begin the discussion by telling the class about his or her job search experiences. For example, the teacher might tell the class how he or she found his or her first job. Have students tell how they found their jobs (through the newspaper, friend, or temporary agency).

Topic 2: New Job

Vocabulary

benefits— payment by employers for services for employees

personnel manager—a person who hires workers and explains benefits

retirement benefits—payment by employers for services for retired employees

safety glasses—special glasses with lenses that protect an employee's eyes from accidents

safety gloves—special gloves that protect an employee's hands

safety shoes—special shoes that protect a person's feet from accidents

shift—a period of work (For example, first shift is 7:00 in the morning to 3:00 in the afternoon; second shift is 3:00 in the afternoon to 11:00 at night, and third shift is 11:00 at night to 7:00 in the morning.)

supervisor—a person who watches over an employee's work

through—finished

Jarad's first day of work as a janitor at Comfort Furniture was good. He worked first shift, 7:00 in the morning to 3:00 in the afternoon. When he arrived at the plant, he talked with the personnel manager, Mr. Smith, who explained health and retirement benefits. Next, Jarad talked with Henry, his supervisor. Henry showed Jarad around the plant and told him what his duties would be. Jarad also met the other members of the janitorial crew. Then, Jarad put on his safety gloves, glasses, and shoes to prevent him from being hurt. Afterward, he began sweeping the floor of the factory. The time passed quickly. Soon it was 3:00 in the afternoon, and he was through for the day. Jarad knew he would enjoy working at Comfort Furniture.

EXERCISE A: Answer the following questions on the lines below.

1. What did the personnel manager and Jarad discuss?

   _____

   _____

   _____

2. Who is Jarad's supervisor?

   _____

   _____

   _____

3. Why is safety clothing important in a factory?

   _____

   _____

   _____

4. In your opinion, did Jarad have a good first day at work?

   _____

   _____

   _____

EXERCISE B: Identify the following word groups as being a sentence or a fragment by writing S (sentence) or F (fragment) in the blank provided. The first one has been done as an example for you.

___F___   1.   When he arrived at the plant.

_____   2.   Jarad talked with Henry, his supervisor.

_____   3.   Who explained health and retirement benefits.

_____   4.   Jarad met the other members of the janitorial crew.

_____   5.   Sweeping the floor of the factory.

_____   6.   The time passed quickly.

Discussion

Have students discuss their first day of their present/most recent job. Students should consider how their feelings about their first day of class are like their feelings on their first day of work.

Topic 3: Worry

Vocabulary

basic skills—reading, writing, or math skills needed to do a job

bonus—extra pay

bought—the past tense of *buy* (In business, one company may buy, or take ownership of, another company.)

on-site—located within a business

president—a person who is in charge of a company or who is the head of a company

release time—time away from a job for which an employee is paid (For example, release time may be given for an employee to have lunch with his or her child at school or to take a class such as English as a Second Language.)

When Yin International bought Silver Fabric, Tran worried about losing her job. Her supervisor told all his employees that they would keep their jobs. Despite her supervisor's words of comfort, Tran worried. Then, early Monday morning, the president of Yin met with all the employees. He told them they could continue to work for the company, and he would like them to improve their job skills. He said employees would be given release time away from their jobs to attend basic skills classes in reading, math, and English as a Second Language, and employees would receive a $500 bonus for each class they completed. He went on to say that an on-site day-care center would be opened for employees' children. Tran was pleased. She knew working for Yin International would be good, and she would no longer have to worry.

EXERCISE A: Answer the following questions on the lines below. The first one has been done as an example for you.

1. Name some problems people face when their company has a new owner.

   Some people get more pay while others have a change in their benefits.

   _____

   _____

2. Name the three basic skills classes that will be offered to employees.

   _____

   _____

   _____

3. What are the new owner's feelings toward the employees?

   _____

   _____

   _____

4. In your opinion, should Tran feel pleased?

_____

_____

_____

EXERCISE B: Identify the following word groups as being a sentence or a fragment by writing S (sentence) or F (fragment) in the blank provided. The first one has been done as an example for you.

___S___ 1. Tran worried about losing her job.

_____ 2. When Yin International bought Silver Fabric.

_____ 3. That they could keep their jobs.

_____ 4. Tran was pleased.

_____ 5. Attended basic skills classes in reading, math, and English as a Second Language.

_____ 6. That an on-site daycare center would be opened.

Discussion

Today many business publications indicate that an individual no longer has the same job for life. Have students discuss how this statement applies to them. The instructor may wish to invite a speaker from a college's Career Development Office or from an outplacement firm to discuss preparing for layoffs.

Topic 4: Community Service

Vocabulary

corporate—a word referring to a large business

higher education—college

internship—job at which a student uses skills learned in college

quarter—a twelve-week period when classes are held. There are four quarters in the school year (fall, winter, spring, and summer).

safety bars—a metal bar that keeps an older person from falling. Safety bars are usually placed in a bathroom.

scholarship—money a student is given to pay for college

team—a group of people

Community involvement is important to Amick Hosiery. Amick employees are divided into four teams. One team builds homes for Habitat for Humanity, and another team puts in safety bars in the homes of elderly people. Teams three and four serve as reading buddies for elementary school students. The company is also involved in the Cities in Schools program, which helps teenagers who are in trouble at school. Another of Amick's interests is higher education. The company gives scholarships at Mayfield Community College. Each quarter five Mayfield machinery students are given internships at Amick. Upon graduation, each intern will be given a job at Amick. The company feels employees who have an education are better trained for their jobs. Amick believes community involvement makes a better employee, and, in turn, the employee becomes a better role model.

EXERCISE A: Answer the following questions on the lines below.

1. Give examples of businesses in your area that are involved in community activities.

   _____

   _____

   _____

2. Why is community involvement important to Amick?

   _____

   _____

   _____

3. Why is education important to Amick?

_____

_____

_____

4. How does Amick feel about its employees?

_____

_____

_____

EXERCISE B: Identify the following word groups as being a sentence or a fragment by writing S (sentence) or F (fragment) in the blank provided. The first one has been done as an example for you.

___S___   1. Community involvement is important to Amick Hosiery.

_____   2. Puts safety bars in the homes of elderly people.

_____   3. Who are in trouble in school.

_____   4. Involved in Cities in Schools Program.

_____   5. Believes community involvement makes a better employee.

_____   6. The employee becomes a better role model.

Discussion

Have students discuss ways their employers are involved in their community. Ask if any students work for companies that have partnerships with public schools or sponsor charity events. The instructor may wish to invite a speaker from a college's financial aid office or a company president to explain the benefits of corporate giving.

SIMPLE SENTENCES—READING

ANSWER KEY

Topic 1
Exercise A:

1. Answers will vary.
2. Answers will vary.
3. Answers will vary.
4. Answers will vary.

Exercise B:

1.	S	2.	F	3.	S
4.	F	5.	F	6.	S

Topic 2
Exercise A:

1. The personnel manager and Jarad discussed health and retirement benefits.
2. Jarad's supervisor is Henry.
3. Safety clothing will prevent an employee from being hurt on the job.
4. Answers will vary.

Exercise B:

1.	F	2.	S	3.	F
4.	S	5.	F	6.	S

Topic 3
Exercise A:

1. Some people get more pay while others have a change in their benefits.
2. The three basic skills classes are reading, math, and English as a Second Language.
3. The new owner is very interested in seeing the employees improve themselves.
4. Answers will vary.

Exercise B:

1.	S	2.	F	3.	F
4.	S	5.	F	6.	F

Topic 4

Exercise A:

1. Answers will vary.
2. Amick believes community involvement makes a better employee.
3. Amick feels employees who have an education are better trained for their jobs.
4. Amick wants its employees to become involved in the community.

Exercise B:

1.	S	2.	F	3.	F
4.	F	5.	F	6.	S

LISTENING

Topic 1: Finding a Job

Vocabulary

applicant—a person who applies for a job

benefits—payment by employers for services for employees

GED—abbreviation for General Equivalency Diploma. A GED is accepted in place of a high school diploma by many employers.

green card—a card issued by the government that lets a person from another country live in the United States as a permanent resident.

interview—questions asked by a personnel manager to a job applicant

job application—a form completed by a job applicant. The form asks for the applicant's name, where the applicant has worked, and where the applicant went to school. Another name for a job application is an Application for Employment.

pay—money an employer gives a worker for doing a job. Workers are paid by the week, every two weeks, or by the month.

personnel manager—a person who hires workers for a company. Another name for a personnel manager is a human resources manager.

personnel office—an office in a company where a person can apply for a job. This office is also called human resources or an employment office.

social security number—a number given by the government to each person; used as a form of identification.

want ad—a written notice in a newspaper about a job that is open. The advertisement will tell the person how to apply for the job and the skills needed for the job.

The following exercises will guide you through the process of finding a job.

EXERCISE A: Listen as your teacher or partner reads the following classified advertisement and answer the questions.

Circulation Assistant

The Greenbriar Public Library is seeking a Circulation Assistant. Duties include: checking out books, processing and shelving books that have been returned, and giving out library cards. Applicants must have a high school diploma or a GED and two years' experience, and must be able to type 35 words per minute. Applicants should have good speaking, reading, and math skills. Pay is $6.90 per hour. Applications will be accepted between 12 noon and 5:00 in the afternoon at the Greenbriar City Hall Personnel Office. All applicants must take a filing and a typing test at the interview. Benefits include health and dental insurance, retirement, and tuition assistance. The City of Greenbriar is an equal opportunity/affirmative action employer.

1. What duties will the circulation assistant perform?

   _____

2. How many years of experience are required for the job?

   _____

3. Name the tests the person will have to take before being hired.

   _____

4. How many words per minute will the person have to type?

   _____

5.   Where are applications accepted?

_____

6.   What type of education should the person have?

_____

EXERCISE B: Place the following information in the correct place on the job application. Some information has already been supplied for you.

Sun Yin   High Point

212-15-6666   October 15, 1960

(336) 555-6630   Wong High School

Saigon College   Teaching

Little Ones Preschool   15 New Street

Helped in the two-year-old classroom   27261

May 1993 - Present   North Carolina

Circulation Assistant

CITY OF GREENBRIAR

APPLICATION FOR EMPLOYMENT

Name: _____ Social Security Number: _____

Position: _____

Address: _____

City: _____ State: _____ Zip Code: _____

Telephone: _____

Are you a United States citizen? _____Yes ___X___ No   Date of Birth:_____

Are you a resident alien? ___X___Yes _____ No

Education: High School: _____

College:_____ Degree: _____

Employment: Company Name: AMA'S Restaurant _____

Duties: Wait tables _____

Dates of Employment: January 1993 – May 1993 _____

Company Name: Lamb's Nursing Home _____

Duties: Helped elderly patients get in and out of bed _____

Dates of Employment: January 1992 – December 1992 _____

Company Name: _____

Duties: _____

Dates of Employment: _____

EXERCISE C: Complete the following Application for Employment by supplying your own information.

APPLICATION FOR EMPLOYMENT

Name: _____ Social Security Number: _____

Position: _____

Address: _____

City: _____ State: _____ Zip Code: _____

Telephone: _____

Are you a United States citizen? _____Yes _____ No   Date of Birth: _____

Are you a resident alien? _____Yes _____ No

Education: High School: _____

                College:_____ Degree: _____

Employment: Company Name: _____

                Duties: _____

                Dates of Employment: _____

                Company Name: _____

                Duties: _____

                Dates of Employment: _____

                Company Name: _____

                Duties: _____

                Dates of Employment: _____

EXERCISE D: Below is a dialogue between a personnel manager and Sun Yin for the position of circulation assistant. Read the dialogue orally with a classmate. Then answer the questions that follow.

PERSONNEL MANAGER: Good morning, Miss Yin.

SUN YIN: Good morning.

PERSONNEL MANAGER: I received your application for the position of circulation assistant.

SUN YIN: I'm very interested in the job. I was a teacher in Vietnam. I love books.

PERSONNEL MANAGER: You have a green card, don't you?

SUN YIN: Yes, I do.

PERSONNEL MANAGER: How long have you lived in the United States?

SUN YIN: Five years.

PERSONNEL MANAGER: You passed our typing and filing tests.

SUN YIN: I'm glad.

PERSONNEL MANAGER: Have you ever worked in a library?

SUN YIN: Yes. I worked one summer in the library in my hometown in Vietnam shelving books.

PERSONNEL MANAGER: Can you work evenings and weekends?

SUN YIN: Yes. I'm very anxious to get back into library work. When can I expect to hear something?

PERSONNEL MANAGER: I'll call you next week. Thank you for your time.

1.   Who is interviewing Sun Yin?

_____

2.   Name the position for which she is being interviewed.

_____

3. What did Sun Yin do in Vietnam?

    _____

4. Does Sun Yin have any library experience?

    _____

5. Does Sun Yin have a green card?

    _____

6. How long has Sun Yin lived in the United States?

    _____

7. When will Sun Yin know if she got the job?

    _____

Discussion

Discuss your most recent job interview with another student and respond to the following questions.

1. Name the job for which you were interviewed.

2. Who interviewed you?

3. What questions did the interviewer ask you?

4. How long did the interview last?

5. Did you have to take any tests?

6. How did you feel after the interview?

Topic 2: The Application for Employment Paragraph

Many times an employer will ask a job applicant to write a paragraph on his or her Application for Employment. The paragraph gives reasons for the applicant's wanting to work for the company. The paragraph should have complete sentences that begin with a capital letter and end with a period. The sentences should have one subject and one verb. There should be no fragments. Personnel officials use this writing to test the applicant's thinking, writing, and sentence skills.

Example:

I want to work for Andre's Pasta. It makes good pasta products. Made pasta in Italy for a living. Like to use my skills in the United States. Like to come to work for Andre's Pasta.

EXERCISE: Listen as your teacher or partner reads the Application for Employment Paragraph. Identify the word groups that are not sentences and do not contain one subject and one verb. Rewrite the paragraph on the lines below, making sure that each word group is a complete sentence and that there are no fragments.

SIMPLE SENTENCES—LISTENING

ANSWER KEY

Topic 1
Exercise A:

1. The duties the circulation assistant will perform are: checking out books, processing and shelving books, and giving out library cards.
2. The job requires two years' experience.
3. The person will have to take a filing and a typing test.
4. The person will have to type 35 words per minute.
5. Applications are accepted at the Greenbriar City Hall Personnel Office.
6. The person must have a high school diploma or a GED.

Exercise B:

CITY OF GREENBRIAR

APPLICATION FOR EMPLOYMENT

Name: Sun Yin   Social Security Number: 212-15-666

Position: Circulation Assistant

Address: 15 New Street

City: High Point   State: North Carolina   Zip Code: 27261

Telephone: (336) 555-6630

Are you a United States citizen? _____ Yes __X__ No   Date of Birth: October 15, 1960

Are you a resident alien? __X__ Yes _____ No

Education: High School: Wong High School

College: Saigon College   Degree: Teaching

Employment: Company Name: Little Ones Preschool

Duties: Helped in the two-year-old classroom

Dates of Employment: May 1993 – Present

Company Name: AMA'S Restaurant

Duties: Wait tables

Dates of Employment: January 1993 – May 1993

Company Name: Lamb's Nursing Home

Duties: Helped elderly patients get in and out of bed

Dates of Employment: January 1992 – December 1992

Exercise C:

The student will supply personal information about himself or herself in this exercise.

Exercise D:

1. The personnel manager is interviewing Sun Yin.
2. Sun Yin is being interviewed for the circulation assistant position.
3. Sun Yin was a teacher in Vietnam.
4. Yes. Sun Yin worked one summer in a library in Vietnam.
5. Yes. Sun Yin has a green card.
6. Sun Yin has lived in the United States for five years.
7. The personnel manager will contact Sun Yin next week.

Topic 2
Exercise:

Answers will vary.

ACTIVITIES

Activity 1: Dramatization

Vocabulary

dialogue—words spoken by actors and actresses in a film

script—printed words actors and actresses speak in a film

video—a film for teaching or entertainment purposes

EXERCISE: You have been asked to write a script for a five (5) minute videotape on a job interview. (There should be one page of dialogue for each minute of video.) Students should work in pairs to compose the dialogue for the company president and for the job applicant. Interview questions and responses should focus on the following points:

> employment history
>
> education
>
> skills
>
> resident status
>
> job title
>
> job duties
>
> benefits

Instructors may wish to invite someone from a college's learning resources center to videotape students performing their dialogue. The interviews should be shown to the class for critiquing and feedback.

Activity 2: Presentation

Vocabulary

business librarian—a person with a degree in library science who knows a lot about the business world business research department—place within a library that provides information about business, such as finding a job or individual businesses in the area

library—a place that has information on all subjects, such as animals or famous people

research—to learn about a subject

EXERCISE: Today, when a person is seeking a job at a company, he or she should research the company. Select a company where you would like to work. Go to your local public library's business research department. Ask the business librarian to help you discover the following information about your company. The Internet is another way of doing research, though great care must be taken to ensure that your sources are trustworthy.

1.   When was the company founded?

2.   How many people does the company employ?

3.   What does the company make?

4.   Who is the president of the company?

5.   How much money did the company earn last year?

Present your findings to the class and explain why you would like to work there.

Activity 3: Art

Students should work in groups of four to create a poster depicting how to find a job in their town. Draw illustrations of various places of business in the town and of people performing different jobs. The text should include names, addresses, and telephone numbers of agencies that can help a person find a job. The instructor may wish to display the students' posters in the classroom.

Activity 4: Writing (select one)

1. Imagine you are a personnel manager. Write a classified advertisement for a cook to work in your company cafeteria. You must include the skills and education the person will need as well as hours, pay, and benefits.

2. Imagine you are a public relations official for a company. Write an announcement of a new employee being hired. You must include the person's name, job title, experience, education, and community activities.

3. Imagine you are the information official for your city. Write a press release (a paragraph that tells about something that is going to happen) about a company relocating to your town. You must include the company's name, where it will be located, what the company will make, and how many people the company will employ.

4. Imagine you are an applicant for the position of customer service representative at Database Technologies. Your application asks you to write a paragraph about your career goals. Write the paragraph, and have your instructor review it for complete sentences.

5. Imagine you are employed in the personnel office of a large business. Your job is to write the employee handbook. Write the section on qualities of a good worker.

6. Imagine you are an employee who has not had a pay increase in two years. Write a letter to your supervisor asking him or her for a pay increase. The letter should include how long you have worked at the company and your reasons for wanting a pay increase.

REVIEW

Key Points

1. A simple sentence expresses a complete thought.

2. The four types of simple sentences are declarative, imperative, interrogative, and exclamatory.

3. A simple sentence begins with a capital letter and ends with either a period, question mark, or exclamation point.

4. A simple sentence has one subject and one verb.

5. A verb phrase has a helping verb and a main verb.

6. Linking Verbs link the subject to a descriptive word.

7. Simple sentences follow four basic patterns.
   Subject + Verb
   Subject + Verb + Direct Object
   Subject + Verb + Indirect Object + Direct Object
   Subject + Linking Verb + Subject Complement

8. A fragment does not express a complete thought.

9. A fragment lacks a subject, a verb, or both.

10. Some common types of fragments are a noun phrase, a prepositional phrase, a verb phrase, and a subordinate phrase.

EXERCISE A: Identify the following sentences as being declarative, imperative, interrogative, or exclamatory. The first one has been done as an example for you.

1. Where is the supervisor?   _____Interrogative_____

2. The third shift begins at 11:00 at night.   _____

3. When will Harry be called back to work?   _____

4. That was a great speech.   _____

5. Do not touch the hot metal!   _____

6. I will be getting a pay increase next month.   _____

EXERCISE B: Begin and end the following sentences correctly. The first one has been done as an example for you.

1. when will the office open

    When will the office open? _____

2. the employment office accepts applications on Tuesdays and Thursdays

    _____

3. do not touch that dye

    _____

4. what time will the meeting be held

    _____

5. safety rules are posted on the walls

    _____

6. how many employees will the company have to hire to fill the order

    _____

EXERCISE C: Identify the subject and verb in each sentence by writing S above the subject and V above the verb. The first one has been done as an example for you.

         S   V

1. Our employees have a good safety record.

2. The new factory will employ 100 people.

3. Johann runs the finishing room.

4. I will be working a double shift tomorrow.

5. Employee Appreciation Day is Friday.

6. Mikos is excited about his new job.

EXERCISE D: Identify the pattern in the following sentences. The patterns are listed below. The first one has been done as an example for you.

A. S + V
B. S + V + DO
C. S + V + IO + DO
D. S + LV + SC

_____D_____ 1. Phey Thong is the new personnel manager.

_____ 2. Hong works at the video store on the weekends.

_____ 3. Mr. Smith is the new president of Shields Decorative Glass.

_____ 4. The maintenance crew gave the employees new recycling bins.

_____ 5. High winds destroyed the sign.

_____ 6. Employees can purchase company stock.

EXERCISE E: Identify the following word groups as being a sentence or a fragment by writing S (sentence) or F (fragment) in the blank provided. The first two have been done as examples for you.

__F__   1. Going to the library.

__S__   2. Sally is studying for her science test.

_____   3. Thursday at 3:00 in the afternoon.

_____   4. While I was at the grocery store.

_____   5. In a cabin in the woods.

_____   6. Tamicka jogs five miles a day.

_____   7. Henri missed the discussion on fragments because he was late for class.

_____   8. Serge has lived in the United States for five years.

SIMPLE SENTENCES—REVIEW

ANSWER KEY

Exercise A:

1. Interrogative
2. Declarative
3. Interrogative
4. Declarative
5. Exclamatory
6. Declarative

Exercise B:

1. When will the office open?
2. The employment office accepts applications on Tuesdays and Thursdays.
3. Do not touch that dye!
4. What time will the meeting be held?
5. Safety rules are posted on the walls.
6. How many employees will the company have to hire to fill the order?

Exercise C:

```
           S        V
```
1. Our employees have a good safety record.
```
           S        V
```
2. The new factory will employ 100 people.
```
       S    V
```
3. Johann runs the finishing room.
```
    S       V
```
4. I will be working a double shift tomorrow.
```
                  S           V
```
5. Employee Appreciation Day is Friday.
```
      S       V
```
6. Mikos is excited about his new job.

Exercise D:

1. D
2. B
3. C
4. C
5. B
6. B

Exercise E:

1. F
2. S
3. F
4. F
5. F
6. S
7. S
8. S

ESL

BEGINNER

CHAPTER 5
Compound Sentences

Chapter 5

COMPOUND SENTENCES

GRAMMAR

Compound Sentence

A **compound sentence** is made up of two or more independent clauses that are connected by one or more coordinating conjunctions and a comma. The first word of the second independent clause is not capitalized.

Example:

The wind was strong, and the tree fell down.

The wind was strong is an independent clause.

And is a conjunction.

The tree fell down is the second independent clause (*the* is not capitalized).

Example:

The man wanted to go shopping, but the store was closed.

The man wanted to go shopping is an independent clause.

But is a conjunction.

The store was closed is the second independent clause (*the* is not capitalized).

Independent Clause

An **independent clause** is a group of words that has a subject and a verb. An independent clause can stand alone as a sentence. When it stands alone as a sentence, it is called a **simple sentence**.

Example:

The wind was strong, and the tree fell down.

The wind was strong is an independent clause. *Wind* is the subject. *Was* is the verb.

The tree fell down is an independent clause. *Tree* is the subject. *Fell* is the verb.

Example:

The man wanted to go shopping, but the store was closed.

The man wanted to go shopping is an independent clause. *Man* is the subject. *Wanted* is the verb.

The store was closed is an independent clause. *Store* is the subject. *Was closed* is the verb.

Conjunctions

Coordinating Conjunctions and Their Meanings

Conjunction	Meaning	Example	Explanation
and	in addition, also	Tom works in sales, **and** Carlos works in accounting.	**And** connects the independent clauses *Tom works in sales* and *Carlos works in accounting.* **And** shows "in addition."
but	except, yet, unless	Tom works in sales, **but** Carlos works in advertising.	**But** connects the independent clauses *Tom works in sales* to *Carlos works in advertising.* **But** shows yet.
for	because	Anna stayed home, **for** she was not feeling well.	**For** gives a reason for Anna staying home: She was not feeling well.
nor	and not, and not either	Miguel did not stand when the teacher walked into the room, **nor** when the teacher left the room.	**Nor** connects the independent clause *Miguel did not stand when the teacher entered the room* to the phrase *when the teacher left the room.* **Nor** means not either.
or	a choice	The children can ride the bus to school, **or** walk.	**Or** shows the students have a choice: riding the bus or walking.
so	therefore	Hugo was tired, **so** he went to bed early.	**So** shows that Hugo was tired; therefore, he went to bed early.
yet	however	The time was not even six o'clock, **yet** it was dark.	**Yet** shows the first independent clause *the time was not even six o'clock* when it was dark.

EXERCISE A: Determine if each sentence is a simple sentence or a compound sentence by writing S (simple sentence) or C (compound sentence) in the blank provided. The first one has been done as an example for you.

___S___   1. The car needed more gas.

_____   2. The dog barked, and the cat meowed.

_____   3. Everybody went home early.

_____   4. Tuan and Tran are cousins.

_____   5. Marie wanted to go on a vacation, but she did not have enough money.

_____   6. My boss said that I was a good employee, and he was happy that he had hired me.

EXERCISE B: Read each compound sentence. Draw one line under the subject of each independent clause. Draw two lines under the verb of each independent clause. Circle the conjunction. The first one has been done as an example for you.

1.   The lightning lit up the sky, and the rain fell.

2.   Jorge rented an apartment on Monday, and he moved into it on Thursday.

3.   Christie wanted to learn to drive, but she did not have a car.

4.   Neither Mark nor Juan can come to the party, but Pierre and Pedro will be there.

5.   My sister works as a waitress, and my brother works as a taxi cab driver.

6.   I work hard at my job, and I am tired at the end of the day.

EXERCISE C: Read each simple sentence. Use a conjunction to form a compound sentence. Write the compound sentence. The first one has been done as an example for you.

1.   The children can play baseball. They cannot play soccer.

   The children can play baseball, but they cannot play soccer.

   _____

2.   The music was very loud. I could not hear what you were saying.

   _____

   _____

3.   Chantel wanted to play outside. Her mother said that she had to stay inside.

   _____

   _____

4.   Be careful as you walk. You will fall into the hole in the ground.

   _____

   _____

5.   Tomika and Carla are friends. They go to the same school.

   _____

   _____

6.   The library was closed. I could not borrow the book I wanted to read.

   _____

   _____

Punctuation

A compound sentence begins and ends just like a simple sentence. A compound sentence can also be declarative, interrogative, or exclamatory. (See chapter 4.)

A compound sentence begins with a **capital letter.**

Example:

The girl went home, and the boy stayed at school.

A compound sentence ends with a **period** (.) if it is a declarative sentence (states something).

Example:

The woman is thirty years old, and the man is twenty-seven years old.

A compound sentence ends with a **question mark(?)** if it is an interrogative sentence (asks something).

Example:

Will you come to my house, or should I come to your house**?**

A compound sentence ends with an **exclamation point** (!) if it is an exclamatory sentence (expresses strong feeling).

Example:

The house is on fire, and the people are screaming!

A **comma** (,) separates parts of a sentence. A comma is used within a sentence when a slight pause or breath is needed. The comma tells the reader to slow down.

Examples:

After 10:00 in the evening, it is too late to call.

Although it is only 4:00 in the afternoon, it is dark outside.

After 10:00 in the evening and *Although it is only 4:00 in the afternoon* are subordinate clauses. A comma is needed after a subordinate clause begins a sentence.

In a compound sentence, a **comma** is used to separate two independent clauses connected by a coordinating conjunction.

Example:

The wind was strong, and the tree fell down.

Example:

Tom and Carlos are friends, but they do not see each other often.

A comma is also used to separate words in a series (words that follow one another).

Example:

It was a nasty, cold, windy day.

Example:

Marie wore a beautiful, long-sleeved, silk, black gown to the party.

Example:

Su-Ming, Linda, Helen, and Anne work at the same factory.

EXERCISE D: Read each compound sentence. End punctuation is missing. Decide if the sentence is declarative, imperative, interrogative, or exclamatory and punctuate correctly. The first one has been done as an example for you.

1.   The waiter was carrying a tray full of food, and he slipped.

2.   The weather turned cold, and the leaves fell off the trees

3.   Do you plan to go to the movies with Mike, or are you going with Robert

4.   Stop crying, and go to your room

5.   Watch out for that large hole or you will fall into it

6.   The bell rang, and all of the workers took a 15-minute break

EXERCISE E: Read each sentence. Each sentence is missing one or more commas. Rewrite each sentence, putting a comma where needed. The first one has been done as an example for you.

1. January February March and April are the first four months of the year.

   January, February, March, and April are the first four months of the year.

2. Pedro is thirty-nine years old 5 feet 7 inches tall and weighs 177 pounds.

3. Every Saturday, my mother goes to the supermarket and buys fresh fruits vegetables and meat.

4. Are you going to the library to get a book written in English or will your father get it for you on his way home from work?

5. John loves animals and he has three cats one bird four goldfish and two dogs.

6. I am tired and need a vacation but I do not have any extra money.

7. Boris wanted to ask Lara to go out with him on a date but he was afraid.

    _____

    _____

8. She wants to become a citizen of the United States but she has not been in the
    country long enough.

    _____

    _____

COMPOUND SENTENCES—GRAMMAR

ANSWER KEY

Exercise A:

1. S   2. CS   3. S
4. S   5. CS   6. CS

Exercise B:

1. The <u>lightning</u> <u>lit</u> up the sky, ⟨and⟩ the <u>rain</u> <u>fell</u>.

2. <u>Jorge</u> <u>rented</u> an apartment on Monday, ⟨and⟩ he <u>moved</u> into it on Thursday.

3. <u>Christie</u> <u>wanted</u> to learn to drive, ⟨but⟩ she <u>did</u> not <u>have</u> a car.

4. Neither <u>Mark nor Juan</u> <u>can come</u> to the party, ⟨but⟩ <u>Pierre and Pedro</u> <u>will be</u> there.

5. My <u>sister</u> <u>works</u> as a waitress, ⟨and⟩ my <u>brother</u> <u>works</u> as a taxi cab driver.

6. <u>I</u> <u>work</u> hard at my job, ⟨and⟩ <u>I</u> <u>am tired</u> at the end of the day.

Exercise C:

1. The children can play baseball, but they cannot play soccer.
2. The music was very loud, so I could not hear what you were saying.
3. Chantel wanted to play outside, but her mother said that she had to stay inside.
4. Be careful as you walk, or you will fall into the hole in the ground.
5. Tomika and Carla are friends, and they go to the same school.
6. The library was closed, so I could not borrow the book I wanted to read.

Exercise D:

1. The waiter was carrying a tray full of food, and he slipped.
2. The weather turned cold, and the leaves fell off the trees.
3. Do you plan to go to the movies with Mike, or are you going with Robert?
4. Stop crying, and go to your room!
5. Watch out for that large hole, or you will fall into it!
6. The bell rang, and all of the workers took a 15-minute break.

Exercise E:

1. January, February, March, and April are the first four months of the year.
2. Pedro is thirty-nine years old, 5 feet 7 inches tall, and he weighs 177 pounds.
3. Every Saturday, my mother goes to the supermarket and buys fresh fruits, vegetables, and meat.
4. Are you going to the library to get a book written in English, or will your father get it for you on his way home from work?
5. John loves animals, and he has three cats, one bird, four goldfish, and two dogs.
6. I am tired and need a vacation, but I do not have any extra money.
7. Boris wanted to ask Lara to go out with him on a date, but he was afraid.
8. She wants to become a citizen of the United States, but she has not been in the country long enough.

VISUALIZING PICTURES

Neighborhood Park

People are having fun at the park.

1. bench	7. jungle gym	12. bike rider
2. trash can	8. water fountain	13. vendor
3. playground	9. swings	14. hand truck
4. sandbox	10. jogger	15. building
5. slide	11. pond	16. carousel
6. seesaw		

EXERCISE A: Look at the picture. Find each numbered item. Think to yourself what the English word is for that item. Look at the words listed below the picture to find out if you knew the correct word. Study the items/words you did not know.

EXERCISE B: Look at the picture. Write six simple sentences to describe what you see in the picture. The first one has been done as an example for you.

1.   A girl is drinking from the water fountain.

2.   _____

3.   _____

4.   _____

5.   _____

6.   _____

EXERCISE C: Look at the picture. Write six compound sentences to describe what you see in the picture. (You may combine some of the simple sentences from Exercise B to form compound sentences.) The first one has been done as an example for you.

1.   A girl is drinking from the water fountain, and another girl is on the swings.

_____

2.   _____

_____

3.   _____

_____

4.   _____

_____

5. _____

_____

6. _____

_____

Jigsaw Puzzle

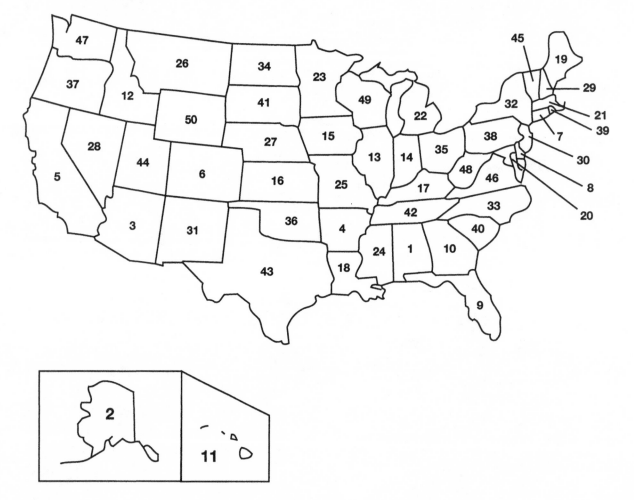

A jigsaw puzzle of the United States has a lot of pieces.

State Name	Abbreviation	State Name	Abbreviation
Alabama	AL	Montana	MT
Alaska	AK	Nebraska	NE
Arizona	AZ	Nevada	NV
Arkansas	AR	New Hampshire	NH
California	CA	New Jersey	NJ
Colorado	CO	New Mexico	NM
Connecticut	CT	New York	NY
Delaware	DE	North Carolina	NC
Florida	FL	North Dakota	ND
Georgia	GA	Ohio	OH
Hawaii	HI	Oklahoma	OK
Idaho	ID	Oregon	OR
Illinois	IL	Pennsylvania	PA
Indiana	IN	Rhode Island	RI
Iowa	IA	South Carolina	SC
Kansas	KS	South Dakota	SD
Kentucky	KY	Tennessee	TN
Louisiana	LA	Texas	TX
Maine	ME	Utah	UT
Maryland	MD	Vermont	VT
Massachusetts	MA	Virginia	VA
Michigan	MI	Washington	WA
Minnesota	MN	West Virginia	WV
Mississippi	MS	Wisconsin	WI
Missouri	MO	Wyoming	WY
		District of Columbia	DC

EXERCISE A: Complete the following chart by filling in the correct abbreviation. You may refer to the list given previously, if needed. The first one has been done as an example for you.

Name of State	Abbreviation
1. Montana	MT
2. Alabama	
3. Hawaii	
4. South Dakota	
5. Illinois	
6. New York	
7. New Jersey	
8. Connecticut	
9. California	

EXERCISE B: Look at the jigsaw puzzle. Write six compound sentences describing the map of the United States. The first one has been done as an example for you.

1. Maine is in the northern part of the country, and Florida is in the southern part of

the country.

2. _____

_____

3. _____

_____

4. _____

_____

5. _____

_____

6. _____

_____

Discussion

Together with a partner, look at a map of the United States and a map of each of your native countries. Discuss how the maps are similar or different. Some things to compare are land size, location near oceans and seas, and the number of states or independent areas in the country.

COMPOUND SENTENCES—VISUALIZING PICTURES

ANSWER KEY

Neighborhood Park
Exercise A

1. bench
2. trash can/garbage can
3. playground
4. sandbox
5. slide
6. seesaw
7. jungle gym
8. water fountain
9. swings
10. jogger
11. pond
12. bike rider
13. vendor
14. hand truck
15. building
16. carousel

Exercise B

Answers will vary.
Here are some examples:
1. A girl is drinking from the water fountain.
2. A person is jogging on the road.
3. The ducks are in the pond.
4. A vendor is selling food.
5. The carousel is next to the building.
6. The sandbox is empty.

Exercise C

Answers will vary.
Here are some examples:
1. A girl is drinking from the water fountain, and another girl is on the swings.
2. A person is jogging on the road, which winds through the park.
3. The ducks are in the pond, which is next to the bench.
4. The bench is empty, and so is the carousel.
5. The carousel is next to the building, which is next to the pond.
6. The sandbox is empty, but the girl riding her bike might stop to play in it.

Jigsaw Puzzle

Exercise A

1.	Montana	MT
2.	Alabama	AL
3.	Hawaii	HI
4.	South Dakota	SD
5.	Illinois	IL
6.	New York	NY
7.	New Jersey	NJ
8.	Connecticut	CT
9.	California	CA

Exercise B:

Answers will vary.

Here are some examples:

1. Maine is in the northern part of the country, and Florida is in the southern part of the country.
2. Arizona borders New Mexico, and New Mexico borders Texas.
3. Hawaii is a series of islands, and it does not border any other states.
4. Washington is north of Oregon, and west of Montana.
5. California borders three states, but none are to the west.
6. Texas is in the middle of the country in the southern part, Minnesota is in the middle of the country in the northern part.

READING

Topic 1: Exercise and Fitness

Vocabulary

aerobics—exercise that helps the heart and lungs

exercise—activities to build up the body

firmer—solid, hard

fitness—a body that is in shape; healthy

gym/fitness center—a place that has exercise equipment

individual—by or for one person

jogging—moving quicker than a walk, but slower than a run

jumping jacks—an exercise where a person jumps and spreads his or her arms and legs apart and jumps again, bringing them together

rollerblading—an activity where a person wears special shoes, each having one row of wheels on the bottom

treadmill—a machine that allows a person to walk in place

All across America, people are becoming more and more interested in their personal health and fitness. They want to feel young, and they want to look young. People exercise to make their muscles stronger and firmer. Some people like to exercise outside, and others like to exercise inside. Some exercises that people can do outside are walking, jogging, bike riding, and rollerblading. They also can play sports such as soccer, baseball, basketball, and tennis. Inside, at home, people often do sit-ups, jumping jacks, and aerobic exercises. Still others like to join gyms and fitness centers. Gym and fitness center memberships are often costly, and not everyone can afford to join. Gyms and fitness centers have employees who have knowledge about exercise, and they make exercise programs that match a person's individual needs. They also show members how to use the many different exercise machines, such as the treadmill and exercise bike. Although the place and type of exercise may be different, exercise has become a part of the lives of many people in America.

EXERCISE A: Answer the following questions on the lines below. The first one has been done as an example for you.

1. In what are more and more people in America becoming interested?

   More and more people are becoming interested in their personal health and

   fitness.

2. Why are they becoming interested in their personal fitness?

3. Where are the different places that people like to exercise?

4. What kinds of exercise do they like to do outside?

5. What are some of the exercises that they can do at home?

6. Why can't all people join a gym or fitness center?

7. Name three things that employees at a gym and fitness center do for their members.

    _____

    _____

EXERCISE B: Within the passage, there are four compound sentences. Write the four compound sentences. The first one has been done as an example for you.

1. They want to feel young, and they want to look young.

    _____

2. _____

    _____

3. _____

    _____

4. _____

    _____

Discussion

Discuss the following questions with a partner.

1. Do you think that exercise should be a regular part of a person's life? Why or why not?

2. In your native country, are people very interested in feeling and looking young? Why or why not? If people exercise, what kinds of exercises do they do? Where and when do they exercise?

3. In your opinion, are Americans too concerned with looking young? Explain.

Topic 2: Education

Vocabulary

college—a school that a person can go to after getting a high school diploma

enroll—to register or sign up for a program or a course of study

graduate—getting a diploma after successfully finishing certain studies

guardian—a person who is not a child's parent, but has legal authority over that child

high school—grades 9 through 12

military—the fighting organizations of the government (Army, Navy, Air Force, Marines)

private school—a school that charges students tuition to maintain itself

public school—a school to which everybody can go because it maintains itself by using money collected from taxes

vocational school—a school where a person can go to learn a particular skill, such as carpentry or welding

In the United States, all children must go to school. It is the law. Children can go to public school, which is free, or their parents or guardians can pay money and send their children to private school. Each state in the country has its own laws about the age at which a child must start going to school. Usually, children begin school when they are five or six years old, and they continue until they are seventeen or eighteen years old. After finishing the twelfth grade, they graduate from high school. Then, they can enroll in college or a vocational school, enter the military, or go to work. Most Americans think getting a good education is important, and they encourage their children to do well in their schoolwork. Often, the more education a person has, the higher paying job he or she can get.

EXERCISE A: Answer the following questions on the lines on the next page. The first one has been done as an example for you.

1. Who must go to school in America?

    All children must go to school in America. _____

    _____

2. If parents or guardians do not want to pay extra money, to what type of school should they send their children?

    _____

    _____

3. For how many years does a child usually go to public or private school?

    _____

    _____

4. After graduating from high school, what can a person do?

    _____

    _____

5. Why do many parents or guardians think that it is important for their child to do well in school?

    _____

    _____

EXERCISE B: Reread Passage 2. Within the reading passage, find three compound sentences. Write each of the compound sentences. Change each compound sentence into simple sentences. An example is done for you.

Example:

The boys walk to school and the girls ride the bus.

a. The boys walk to school.

b. The girls ride the bus.

1. _____

   a. _____

   b. _____

2. _____

   a. _____

   b. _____

3. _____

   a. _____

   b. _____

Discussion

With a partner, discuss your answers to the following questions:

1. Do you think it should be a law that all children must go to school? Explain.

2. Do you think that it is fair that higher paying jobs are often given to people with the most education?

3. In your native country, are there laws about children having to go to school? What are the laws? If your native country does not have these laws, do you think that the country should have laws? Explain.

Topic 3: Planning a Vacation

Vocabulary

activities—things to do

confusion—hard to understand, mixed-up

cruise—a vacation that takes place on a large ship

itineraries—exact travel plans that tell where a person will go and when he or she will be there

reservations—holding of travel plans (airline tickets, hotel rooms, etc.) until ready for use by a person

travel agency—a place where a person can go to get help with travel plans

vacation—a temporary escape from daily activities to rest, to take it easy, and to have fun

Deciding where to go on a vacation is often confusing. There are many things to think about before deciding where to go. How much money will the vacation cost? What kinds of activities can be done at certain places? What type of weather can be expected? Is it better to travel with a group, or is it better to travel alone? Should you stay at one place for the whole time, or should you stay at several places? To help get the answers to these and other questions, a person often goes to a travel agency. It is the business of the travel agency to know this type of information. The travel agency works directly with the airline companies, cruise line companies, train line companies, and hotels, so a person can plan a whole vacation without having to spend hours on the telephone. All reservations and itineraries are arranged by the travel agency. It does not cost a person any extra money to have a travel agency do this for him or her because the travel agency is paid by the airlines, cruise companies, train companies, and hotels. Going to a travel agency is often a good way of taking the confusion out of vacation planning.

EXERCISE A: Answer the following questions on the lines below. The first one has been done as an example for you.

1. Why is planning a vacation often confusing?

   Planning a vacation is often confusing because there are many things to think
   about.

2.   Name five questions that have to be thought about when planning a vacation.

_____

_____

3.   What does a travel agency do?

_____

_____

4.   Why is it often easier to plan a vacation using a travel agency than doing it yourself?

_____

_____

5.   How does a travel agency make money if it does not charge extra money for its services?

_____

_____

EXERCISE B: Decide if the following sentences are simple sentences or compound sentences by writing S (simple sentence) or CS (compound sentence) in the blank provided. The first one has been done as an example for you.

___S___   1.   How much money will the vacation cost?

_____   2.   What kinds of activities can be done at certain places?

_____   3.   Is it better to travel with a group, or is it better to travel alone?

_____   4.   Should you stay at one place for the whole time, or should you stay at several places?

_____   5.   The travel agency works directly with the airlines, cruise companies, train companies, and hotels, so a person can plan a whole vacation without spending hours on the phone.

_____   6.   Going to a travel agency is often a good way of taking the confusion out of vacation planning.

Discussion

With a partner, discuss your answers to the following questions.

1. Have you ever planned a vacation?

2. Did you plan the vacation yourself or did someone help you? Explain.

3. Are there businesses similar to travel agencies in your native country? If yes, do their services cost extra money? If no, do you think this type of business would succeed in your native country? Explain.

Topic 4: American Family Households

Vocabulary

divorce—legal separation of two married people

household—all those living in one house

single parent—a parent who does not have a husband or wife

typical—usual

American Family Households

Family households across America are changing. For many, many years, most households in America had a husband, wife, and children. Grandparents, aunts, uncles, and cousins lived in the same house or they lived close by. Then, slowly, households began to change because family members started moving away. Husbands moved with their wives and children to other cities to take better jobs and to earn more money. Children left home to go to college or vocational school, to enter the military, or to work full-time, and they decided to live in other places. Divorce among couples continues to change households. Households headed by single parents are now very common. Now, in America, there is no such thing as a typical family household. Households have become as different as America itself.

EXERCISE A: Answer the following questions on the lines below.

1. Years ago, who usually lived in one household?

    _____

    _____

2. If grandparents did not live in the same house, where did they live?

    _____

    _____

3. What started the change in households?

    _____

    _____

4. Why did children decide to live in other places?

    _____

    _____

5. What continues to change households?

    _____

    _____

EXERCISE B: Punctuate the following sentences from the passage correctly using commas. An example has been done for you.

Example:

In America, children attend elementary school for five years, middle school for three years, and high school for four years.

1. For many many years most households in America had a husband wife and children.

2. Grandparents aunts uncles and cousins lived in the same house or they lived close by.

3. Husbands moved with their wives and children to other cities to take better jobs and to earn more money.

4. Children left home to go to college or vocational school to enter the military or to work full-time.

Discussion

Form a small group of three or four people, and discuss your ideas about the following:

1. Do you think the change in the American family household is for the better or for the worse?

2. What effect do you think it might have upon the children in these households?

3. Has there also been a change in family households in your native country?

4. How do you feel about this change?

COMPOUND SENTENCES—READING

ANSWER KEY

Topic 1
Exercise A:

1. More and more people are becoming interested in their personal health and fitness.
2. They want to feel and look young.
3. People like to exercise outside and inside.
4. Outside, people like to walk, jog, bike ride, and rollerblade.
5. At home, people can do sit-ups, jumping jacks, and aerobic exercises.
6. All people cannot join a gym and fitness center because they are costly.
7. (a) Employees at a gym and fitness center share their knowledge about exercises.
   (b) Employees at a gym and fitness center make exercise programs that match a person's needs.
   (c) Employees at a gym and fitness center show people how to use the exercise machines.

Exercise B:

1. They want to feel young, and they want to look young.
2. Some people like to exercise outside, and others like to exercise inside.
3. Gym and fitness center memberships are often costly, and not everyone can afford to join.
4. Gyms and fitness centers have employees who have knowledge about exercise, and they make exercise programs that match a person's personal needs.

Topic 2
Exercise A:

1. All children must go to school in America.
2. They should send their child to public school, which is free.
3. A child usually goes to public or private school for 12 years.
4. A person can enroll in college or vocational school, enter the military, or go to work.

5. They think that education is important so that their child can get a good paying job.

Exercise B:

1. Children can go to public school, which is free, or their parents or guardians can pay money and send their children to private school.
    a. Children can go to public school, which is free.
    b. Their parents or guardians can pay money and send their children to private school.
2. Usually, children begin school when they are five or six years old, and they continue until they are seventeen or eighteen years old.
    a. Usually, children begin school when they are five or six years old.
    b. They continue until they are seventeen or eighteen years old.
3. Most Americans think getting a good education is important, and they encourage their children to do well in their schoolwork.
    a. Most Americans think getting a good education is important.
    b. They encourage their children to do well in their school work.

Topic 3

Exercise A:

1. Planning a vacation is often confusing because there are many things to think about.
2. The five questions that have to be thought about when planning a vacation are
    a. How much money will the vacation cost?
    b. What kind of activities can be done?
    c. What type of weather can be expected?
    d. Is it better to travel with a group or alone?
    e. Should one stay at one place the whole time or stay in several places?
3. A travel agency shares information about traveling and plans trips.
4. The travel agency plans everything and the customer does not have to spend hours on the phone.
5. A travel agency is paid by the airlines, cruise companies, train companies, and hotels with which it does business.

Exercise B:

1. S	2. S	3. CS
4. CS	5. CS	6. S

Topic 4

Exercise A:

1. A husband, wife, children and sometimes grandparents, aunts, uncles, and cousins lived in one household.
2. They lived close by.
3. Family members started moving away.
4. They left to go to college or vocational school, to join the military, or to work full-time.
5. Divorce continues to change households.

Exercise B:

1. For many, many years most households in America had a husband, wife, and children.
2. Grandparents, aunts, uncles, and cousins lived in the same house or they lived close by.
3. Husbands moved with their wives and children to other cities to take better jobs and to earn more money.
4. Children left home to go to college or vocational school, to enter the military, or to work full-time.

LISTENING

Topic 1: Fitness Center

Vocabulary

fitness center—a place where people go to exercise

mat—a soft piece of foam that is used when exercising

PART 1: Look at the picture of the fitness center as you listen to your teacher or partner read the following passage.

> The time is 3:00 in the afternoon and the fitness center is busy. An employee is speaking with two people who are interested in joining the fitness center. A woman reads a book as she rides an exercise bike. There are people lying on mats doing floor exercises. There are other people on mats doing exercises to help make their legs stronger and firmer. The fitness center has a weight room and a swimming pool. It is a great place to get into shape if you can afford it!

EXERCISE: Look at the picture of the fitness center on the next page and listen as your teacher or partner gives directions. Follow the directions.

1. Circle the clock. Next to the clock, write the time shown on the clock.

2. Draw a box around the woman on the exercise bike.

3. Write an **X** on the picture of each person lying on a mat doing floor exercises.

4. Circle the weights that the man is using to make his arms stronger.

5. Draw a box around the towel lying near the swimming pool.

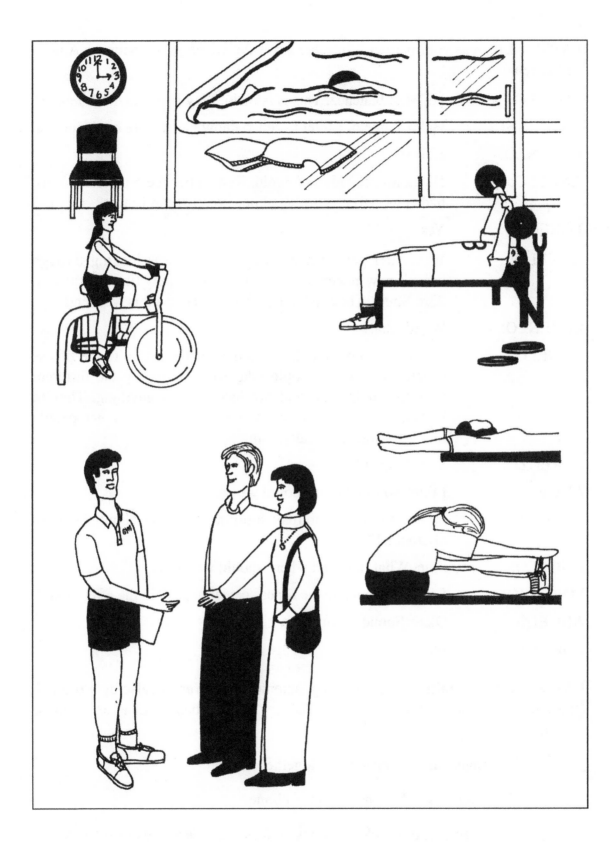

PART 2: Listen as your partner or teacher reads the conversation between Angelo and Lorenzo.

ANGELO: Hi, Mrs. Sanchez. This is Angelo. May I speak with Lorenzo?

MRS. SANCHEZ: Hello, Angelo. I'll let Lorenzo know that you're on the phone.

LORENZO: Hello?

ANGELO: Hi, Lorenzo. This is Angelo. Remember the conversation we had at work this morning about exercise and fitness?

LORENZO: Yes.

ANGELO: Well, after getting home from work, I was looking through today's newspaper and saw an ad for the new fitness center on 23rd Street. They're having an Open House this weekend.

LORENZO: What's that?

ANGELO: An Open House is a time when a person can go to the fitness center, talk to the people who work there, try the different exercise equipment, and not have to pay anything. They're having this Open House as a way of trying to get people interested and, hopefully, join.

LORENZO: Sounds great!

ANGELO: I think so too. When should we go?

LORENZO: I have to work Saturday morning, so how about Saturday afternoon?

ANGELO: Fine. What time and where should we meet?

LORENZO: Let's meet outside the fitness center at 2:00 in the afternoon.

ANGELO: Okay. Sounds good. Bye.

LORENZO: Bye.

EXERCISE: Determine if the following statements are true or false by writing T (true) or F (false) in the blank provided. The first one has been done as an example for you.

___T___   1. Angelo and Lorenzo work together.

_____   2. Lorenzo's father answered the phone.

_____   3. Lorenzo and Angelo should wear a suit and tie to the Open House.

_____ 4. Lorenzo and Angelo are interested in getting into shape.

_____ 5. Angelo and Lorenzo are having this conversation at work.

_____ 6. The Open House is scheduled for the weekend.

_____ 7. Mrs. Sanchez knew Angelo.

_____ 8. Angelo knew about the Open House from hearing an ad on the radio.

Discussion

Form a small group of three or four people. Discuss the answers to the following questions:

Have you ever gone to an Open House? What type of business was it? Did the Open House get you interested enough to spend your money there (buy something, join, etc.)? Do you think having an Open House is a good idea for a business? Explain. What are some of the ways businesses in your native country try to increase business?

Topic 2: School

PART 1: Look at the picture of children starting their school day on the next page as you listen to your teacher or partner read the following passage.

Vocabulary

bus—a vehicle that takes children to school

classroom—room in a school where lessons are taught

school bag—something that contains books, pens, and pencils

The time is 8:30 in the morning, and the school buses are arriving in front of the school building. Children are getting off the buses, and they are walking into the building. A teacher is standing at the front door as the children walk inside. Each boy and girl walks to his or her classroom. Inside their classroom, the boys and girls hang up their coats in the coat closet, empty their school bags, and sit at their desks waiting for directions

from their teacher. The teacher is writing with chalk on the chalkboard. The teacher writes, "Good morning. Today is Thursday. The order of subjects for today is math, social studies, art, reading, writing, and science." The students take out their math books, and the school day begins.

EXERCISE A: Without looking back at the text about the children arriving at school, write the order that things happened. The first two have been done for you.

_____ The children take out their math books.

___2___ The children walk inside the school building.

_____ A teacher stands at the front door as the boys and girls walk inside.

___1___ The children get off the buses.

_____ The boys and girls hang up their coats in the coat closet.

_____ The teacher writes with chalk on the chalkboard.

_____ The children sit at their desks and wait for directions from their teacher.

_____ The children empty their school bags.

PART 2: Listen as your teacher or partner reads the conversation between three people as they stand waiting for a bus to take them to work.

MRS. LINN:	Good morning, Mrs. Chang. Good morning, Mr. Rodriquez.
MRS. CHANG:	Good morning, Mrs. Linn. Nice day, isn't it?
MR. RODRIQUEZ:	Good morning, Mrs. Linn. How are you today?
MRS. LINN:	Not so good. I know that it is the law that all children go to school when they become five or six years old. My son has just had his sixth birthday, and I don't know how to get him into school. I don't want to break the law. What should I do?
MRS. CHANG:	You have to go and register him at your local neighborhood school.
MRS. LINN:	I don't understand. Register?

MRS. CHANG:	Register means to sign him up for school. You'll have to fill out some papers or forms giving information about your son, and then he'll be able to start school.
MR. RODRIQUEZ:	My son, Carlos, started school two months ago. When I went to register him, I had to bring proof that the information I filled out on the forms was true.
MRS. LINN:	Proof? What kind of proof?
MR. RODRIQUEZ:	I had to bring his birth certificate to show that he was the correct age to start school. I also had to bring a telephone bill or a gas or electric bill.
MRS. LINN:	Why?
MR. RODRIQUEZ:	To show proof of residency. To send our son to the public school near our home, I had to show something official to prove that we lived where we said we did, and not in another town. It has something to do with taxes.
MRS. CHANG:	When I signed my daughter up for school, I also remember being asked to show proof of her immunizations.
MRS. LINN:	Immuniza...?
MRS. CHANG:	Immunizations. The shots she received at the clinic to keep her healthy. The doctor at the clinic gave me a piece of paper with this information on it, and I brought it with me when I registered my daughter.
MRS. LINN:	This all sounds very hard!
MRS. CHANG:	No, it isn't. Just bring all this information with you, and you'll have no problem.
MR. RODRIQUEZ:	The people at the school where you register are very nice and will help you as much as they can.
MRS. LINN:	I hope so. Here's the bus. Have a good day.

EXERCISE A: Without looking back at the conversation between Mrs. Linn, Mrs. Chang, and Mr. Rodriquez, match the words in the left column with their explanation in the right column.

1.	neighborhood school	a.	to sign up
2.	register	b.	shots to keep a child healthy
3.	birth certificate	c.	school near where you live
4.	immunizations	d.	proof of a person's age
5.	proof of residency	e.	telephone, gas, or electric bill
6.	public school	f.	gets money from taxes

EXERCISE B: A sample registration form appears below. Complete the form by writing your own information in the correct spaces.

Sample School Registration Form

_____   _____   _____
Student's Last Name   First Name   Middle Initial

_____   _____   _____
Date of Birth   Sex   Place of Birth (Country)

_____   _____
Native Language   Language(s) Spoken at Home

_____   _____   _____   _____
Street   Apt. Number   City   State   Zip Code

_____   _____   _____   _____   _____
School Last Attended   City   State   Country   Grade

_____   _____   _____   _____
Name of Parent/Guardian   Street   City   State

_____   _____
Place of Employment   Area Code Telephone Number

_____   _____
Contact in Case of Emergency   Area Code Telephone Number

Discussion

Form a small group of three or four people. Discuss the answers to the following questions.

1. Have you ever had to register to go to school, to join a team, to join a club, or to join any other group? Explain.

2. What did you have to do or bring with you when you registered?

3. In your native country, do children have to be registered to go to school? If yes, what do you have to do to register the child? If no, do you think children should have to be registered to go to school? Explain.

4. Discuss how you might solve the problem of not having the proper proof of residency or an official birth certificate.

Discussion

With a partner, discuss a family party you either gave or attended. Do you think it is a good idea for entire families to get together? If you do think so, how often do you think they should get together? Why? If you do not think so, why not?

COMPOUND SENTENCES—LISTENING

Topic 1: Fitness Center

Part 1

Exercise:

see illustration on next page

Part 2

Exercise:

1. T	2. F	3. F	4. T
5. F	6. T	7. T	8. F

Topic 2: School

Part 1

Exercise A

8   The children take out their math books.
2   The children walk inside the school building.
3   A teacher stands at the front door as the boys and girls walk inside.
1   The children get off the buses.
4   The boys and girls hang up their coats in the coat closet.
7   The teacher writes with chalk on the chalkboard.
6   The children sit at their desks and wait for directions from their teacher.
5   The children empty their school bags.

Part 2

Exercise A:

1. neighborhood school
2. register
3. birth certificate
4. immunizations
5. proof of residency
6. public school

c. school near where you live
a. to sign up
d. proof of a person's age
b. shots to keep a child healthy
e. telephone, gas, or electric bill
f. gets money from taxes

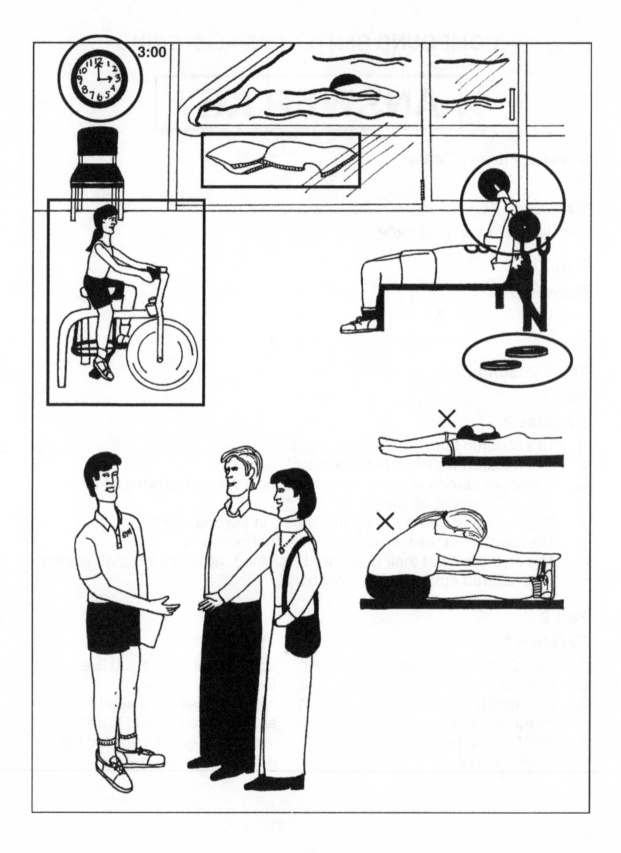

Exercise B:

Answers will vary.

Sample School Registration Form

Rodriguez	Juan	A.
Student's Last Name	First Name	Middle Initial

4-16-67	M	Puerto Rico
Date of Birth	Sex	Place of Birth (Country)

Spanish	Spanish
Native Language	Language(s) Spoken at Home

2 Adams St., #16B	Brooklyn	NY	11235
Street Apt. Number	City	State	Zip Code

Ebbetts High School	Brooklyn	NY	USA	12
School Last Attended	City	State	Country	Grade

Jose Rodriguez	2 Adams St., #16B	Brooklyn	NY
Name of Parent/Guardian	Street	City	State

Cafe Hispania	718-555-7718
Place of Employment	Area Code Telephone Number

Jose Rodriguez	718-555-2346
Contact in Case of Emergency	Area Code Telephone Number

ACTIVITIES

Activity 1: Wordsearch

A wordsearch is a type of puzzle done on paper. Certain words are "hidden" within the puzzle. To find out which words are "hidden" in the puzzle, information is written below the puzzle box. The information is either the words themselves or the definitions of the words. After a "hidden" word has been found within the puzzle, it is circled. A wordsearch is completed after all the "hidden" words have been located and circled. A person can be given a set amount of time to complete the wordsearch or allowed as much time as needed.

Wordsearch

STEP 1: Review the vocabulary words that come before any three reading passages in this book. Select three words from each passage (total: 12 words). On a piece of paper, write each selected word and its definition.

STEP 2: On a piece of paper, draw a large square. Write each of the selected words within the square. These words can be written in any direction. Fill in the spaces around the words with any letters of the alphabet. See example.

STEP 3: Below the square, write the definitions of the selected "hidden" words. These do not have to be written in the same order as you wrote the words in the square. See example.

STEP 4: Exchange wordsearches with a partner and solve! See example.

Vocabulary

firm—solid, hard

enroll—to register or sign-up

divorce—legal separation of two married people

Example

r	e	n	r	o	l	l	d	o	w	n
d	i	v	o	r	c	e	m	a	n	t
f	u	w	o	p	q	a	n	c	o	y
i	a	r	d	x	j	e	e	l	t	i
r	p	o	h	d	f	y	a	u	c	f
m	e	r	s	k	m	t	e	d	g	v

Activity 2: Compound Sentence/Simple Sentence Board Game

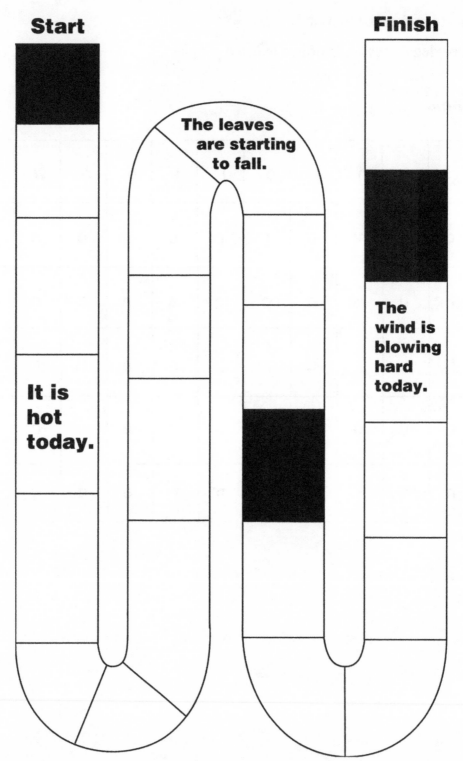

Directions

This activity is best done in small groups of four to six people.

STEP 1: Each member of the group writes three compound sentences and three different simple sentences on a piece of paper. Each member of the group reads his or her sentences to the other members of the group. The group discusses each sentence with regard to its English correctness. Sentences are revised, if necessary.

STEP 2: One person from each group draws the game board outline on a piece of posterboard or large piece of paper. See sample game board outline given on the previous page.

STEP 3: On the game board, each group member writes his or her sentences; one sentence in each box. There should be more boxes on the game board than there are sentences. Separate some of the sentence boxes by having blank boxes between them. See sample.

STEP 4: Using posterboard or heavier paper, cut thirty 3-inch by 3-inch squares.

STEP 5: On the squares, each member of the group writes directions, such as:

Change the subject of the sentence.

Change the sentence into a simple or compound sentence.

Change the sentence using a conjunction.

Change the verb of the sentence.

Etc.

Make some of the squares "fun" cards, such as:

You have won the lottery. Move forward 5 spaces.

You were late for work. Move back 3 spaces.

Your car is broken. Miss one turn.

Etc.

STEP 6: Play the Game!

Materials:

dice

30 game board squares

4 to 6 player markers (anything that can be used to mark each player's spot on the game board as the player moves).

Rules:

1.   Each player tosses the dice to decide who goes first. The person with the highest number is first; the person with the next highest number is second, etc.

2.   The game board squares are put on the game board face-down (no writing showing).

3.   The first player tosses the dice and moves that many spaces on the game board.

4.   If the person moves to a box with a sentence, he or she must pick one game board square and follow the directions. If the person is unable to follow the directions correctly, he or she must move back one space. If the directions are followed correctly, the person stays where he or she is on the game board and waits for their next turn. The game board square is returned to the bottom of the pile.

5.   If the person moves to a blank box, that person gets to toss the dice again and move that number of spaces.

6.   The winner of the game is the person who is the first to move around the entire board to the Finish Box.

NOTE: For variety, each group can exchange their game board set with that of another group and play the new game.

REVIEW

Key Points

1. A compound sentence is made up of two independent clauses joined by a comma and a coordinating conjunction.

2. The coordinating conjunctions are *and, but, for, nor, or,* and *so.*

3. An independent clause has a subject and a verb.

4. A compound sentence begins with a capital letter.

5. A compound sentence ends with a period, a question mark, or an exclamation point.

EXERCISE A: Identify the following sentences as being simple sentences or compound sentences by writing S (simple sentence) or CS (compound sentence) in the blank provided. The first one has been done as an example for you.

_CS_   1. Brian graduated from high school, and he is going to go to college.

_____   2. Mrs. Sanchez is thinking about joining a fitness center.

_____   3. Will you meet me at the fitness center, or will you meet me at home?

_____   4. Mr. and Mrs. Goland are going to the travel agency to plan a vacation.

_____   5. Marie is five years old, and Ben is six years old.

_____   6. Marie's mother and father were born in Spain.

_____   7. Pierre's grandmother lives in the apartment upstairs, and Pierre's uncle lives in the apartment downstairs.

_____ 8. Lorenzo and Angelo are going to the Open House at the fitness center.

_____ 9. There were women at the fitness center lifting weights, and there were men swimming in the swimming pool.

_____ 10. Mrs. Patel registered her son for first grade, and she registered her daughter for third grade.

EXERCISE B: Underline the conjunctions in the following sentences. The first one has been done as an example for you.

1. Thomas is going, <u>but</u> Matt is staying home.

2. Is this for me or for you?

3. Tony is tired, and he is going to sleep.

4. The little girl cried, but she had to go on the school bus.

5. All the lights were on in the house, yet no one was home.

6. Can I come, or do I have to stay home?

7. Neither Hugo nor Jorge had enough money.

8. I will meet you after work, and we can have dinner together.

9. My aunt, uncle, grandmother, and cousin are coming to visit.

10. I want to get into shape, but I hate to exercise.

EXERCISE C: Combine the sentences to make one compound sentence. Write your answer on the lines provided. The first one has been done as an example for you.

1. Marge is a single parent. She has three children.

    Marge is a single parent, and she has three children. _____

    _____

2. Tuan wants to take a vacation. He has no money.

    _____

    _____

3. Is this mine? Is this yours?

    _____

    _____

4. Su-Ming wanted to go to the library. The library was closed.

    _____

    _____

5. The girl was jogging. Her friend was jogging, too.

    _____

    _____

6. The teacher told the class to take out their science books. Stop talking.

    _____

    _____

7. Amit wanted to telephone his friend, Scott. Amit did not know Scott's phone number.

    _____

    _____

8. Mrs. Petrie wanted to register her son for public school. She did not have proof of residency.

    _____

    _____

9. Jack likes to rollerblade in the park. Joe likes to ride his bike.

    _____

    _____

10. George likes ice cream. He hates chocolate candy.

    _____

    _____

COMPOUND SENTENCES—REVIEW

ANSWER KEY

Review

Exercise A:

1. CS	2. S	3. CS	4. S
5. CS	6. S	7. CS	8. S
9. CS	10. CS		

Exercise B:

1. but
2. or
3. and
4. but
5. yet
6. or
7. nor
8. and
9. and
10. but

Exercise C:

1. Marge is a single parent, and she has three children.
2. Tuan wants to take a vacation, but he has no money.
3. Is this mine, or is this yours?
4. Su-Ming wanted to go to the library, but the library was closed.
5. The girl was jogging and her friend was jogging, too.
6. The teacher told the class to take out their science books and stop talking.
7. Amit wanted to telephone his friend, Scott, but Amit did not know Scott's phone number.
8. Mrs. Petrie wanted to register her son for public school, but she did not have proof of residency.
9. Jack likes to roller blade in the park, and Joe likes to ride his bike.
10. George likes ice cream, but he hates chocolate candy.

ESL

BEGINNER

CHAPTER 6

Modification

Chapter 6

MODIFICATION

GRAMMAR

Modifiers

Modifiers are used with other words, such as nouns or pronouns, to make the meaning of a sentence clearer and more exact.

Example:

The dog barks.

Dog is the subject. *The* is the modifier. *The* refers to *dog*.

There are several kinds of modifiers.

Adjectives

An **adjective** refers to a noun, a pronoun, or any other word or group of words playing the part of a noun. Adjectives help to describe or limit nouns.

Example:

Wong is short.

Short is an adjective. *Short* describes the subject *Wong* (noun).

Adjectives can also describe size (big, little, small), appearance (beautiful, handsome), personality (kind, intelligent), color (green, blue), and number (one, two).

Examples:

The kitten is small.

Small is an adjective. *Small* describes the kitten's size.

Gabrielle is a beautiful woman.

Beautiful is an adjective. *Beautiful* describes the woman's appearance.

Garcia is a kind man.

Kind is an adjective. *Kind* describes the man's personality.

The paint is blue.

Blue is an adjective. *Blue* describes the color of the paint.

Two boys played in the sandbox.

Two is an adjective. *Two* describes the number of boys.

Articles

An **article** is a type of adjective. An article comes before a noun. The articles are "a," "an," and "the." There are two kinds of articles — **definite articles** and **indefinite articles**. "The" is a definite article. Definite articles are used to refer to a specific thing, such as "the pen"— a specific pen. "A" and "an" are indefinite articles. Indefinite articles refer to something general, such as "a tree" (any tree). "A" is used before a word that begins with a consonant, such as "a tree" ("t" is a consonant). "An" is used before a word that begins with a vowel, such as "an egg" ("e" is a vowel).

NOTES:

A.   The consonants are "b," "c," "d," "f," "g," "h," "j," "k," "l," "m," "n," "p," "q," "r," "s," "t," "v," "w," "x," "y," and "z."

B.   The vowels are "a," "e," "i," "o," "u," and sometimes "y."

C.   There are several exceptions to the indefinite article rule: Sometimes a word starting with a consonant will use *an* as its article. This occurs when the consonant is silent. Likewise, sometimes a word beginning with a vowel will use *a* as its article because the vowel sounds like a consonant.

Examples:

an hour (The letter "h" is silent.)

a university (The "u" sounds like a "y.")

D.   An article is not used before a plural noun.

Example:

The dogs are friendly animals. (wrong)

Dogs is a plural noun. The article *the* is not needed before a plural noun.

Dogs are friendly animals. (correct)

See Appendix J for more information.

Demonstrative Adjectives

A **demonstrative adjective** refers to a specific noun. The demonstrative adjectives are *this/that* and *these/those.*

This/that is used with a singular noun.

Examples:

This table is for sale.

That table is for sale.

This/that refer to the singular noun *table.*

These/those are used with a plural noun.

Examples:

These tables are for sale.

Those tables are for sale.

These/Those refer to the plural noun *tables.*

Adverbs

An **adverb** refers to a verb, an adjective, or another adverb. Adverbs describe how something happens, when something happens, or how a person does something. Many times an adverb will end in "ly."

Examples:

Susan walked slowly.

Slowly is an adverb. *Slowly* refers to the verb walked. *Slowly* tells how Susan walked. *Slowly* ends in "ly."

Susan is very beautiful.

Very is an adverb. *Very* refers to the adjective beautiful. *Very* tells how beautiful Susan is.

Susan runs fast.

Fast is an adverb. *Fast* refers to the verb runs. *Fast* tells how Susan runs.

NOTES:

A. Some words, such as "hard," "fast," "late," and "early" can be both adjectives and adverbs. If the word refers to a noun, the word is an adjective. If the word refers to an adjective, an adverb, or a verb, the word is an adverb.

Examples:

Yesterday, the bus was late.

Late is an adjective referring to the noun *bus*.

Yesterday, I went to class late.

Late is an adverb referring to the verb *went*.

B. The past participle that you studied in Chapter 2, "Verbs and Verb Phrases," can be used as an adjective.

Example:

The injured child was taken to the hospital.

Injured is a past participle. *Injured* is used as an adjective.

Injured describes *child*.

C. If a demonstrative adjective is not followed by a noun, the demonstrative adjective is called a **demonstrative pronoun** because it takes the place of a noun.

Examples:

This hat is mine. (demonstrative adjective)

This is mine. (demonstrative pronoun)

EXERCISE A: Write "a" before a word that begins with a consonant and "an" before a word that begins with a vowel. The first one has been done as an example for you.

__A__   1. car

_____   2. apple

_____   3. oak tree

_____   4. boat

_____   5. pizza

_____   6. tomato

_____   7. airplane

_____   8. ice cream cone

EXERCISE B: Complete the following sentences by writing "a," "an," or "the" in the blank(s) provided. The first one has been done as an example for you.

1.   How far is it from here to <u>the</u> next town?

2.   Can you turn down _____ television? I am studying.

3.   I am going to take _____ shower after I get off _____ telephone.

4.   What is _____ name of _____ man we met at the party last night?

5.   They live in _____ old house near the town hall. It is a long way from _____ Jones' house.

6.   I love going to _____ university. I am learning so much.

7.   I am going to clean _____ car, write _____ letter, and make _____ telephone call.

EXERCISE C: Underline the demonstrative pronoun that correctly completes the sentence. The first one has been done as an example for you.

1.   (This, <u>These</u>) books belong in the library.

2.   Su Yin is certain (this, those) is her American history book.

3.   You can find (this, those) snow peas in the frozen food section.

4.   Can you be ready to catch (that, those) bus at 7:00 in the morning?

5.   Study (these, that) words carefully for your spelling test.

6.   I like (this, those) stove the best of any I have seen at Sears.

EXERCISE D: Underline the word that correctly completes the following sentences. The first one has been done as an example for you.

1.   These pears are (<u>delicious,</u> deliciously). Try one.

2.   My teacher is very (strict, strictly), and she always gives us a lot of homework.

3.   It is very important to be a (careful, carefully) driver.

4.   Mary was not (good, well) last week, so she stayed home.

5.   She is a seamstress. She sews (beautiful, beautifully).

See Appendix K for more information.

Comparative and Superlative

Adjectives and adverbs can be made to compare people, things, or groups.

The **comparative** form compares two persons, things, or groups. The comparative form is made by adding "er" to words of one syllable or placing the word "more" before the word.

Examples:

Tom is stronger than Joe.

Tom's strength is being compared to Joe's. *Strong* is one syllable. "Er" must be added to *strong* to compare Tom's strength to Joe's.

My computer class is more interesting than my algebra class. Computer class is being compared to algebra class.

Interesting is made up of more than one syllable. "More" must be added before *interesting* to compare computer class to algebra class.

The **superlative** is used to compare more than two people, things, or groups. The superlative is formed by adding "est" to words of one syllable and by placing the word "most" before words of more than one syllable.

Examples:

Today is the hottest day of the summer.

Hot is one syllable. *Hot* is made superlative by adding "est." *Hottest* tells that today is the hottest of all the days in the summer.

Television shows on American history are most interesting. Interesting is made up of more than one syllable.

Interesting is made superlative by placing the word *most* before *interesting*. *Most interesting* tells that television shows on American history are most interesting as compared with all other shows on television.

The following adjectives change spellings in the comparative and superlative forms:

Adjective	Comparative	Superlative
bad	worse	worst
good	better	best
little	less	least
many	more	most

The following adverbs change spellings in the comparative and superlative forms:

Adverb	Comparative	Superlative
badly	worse	worst
much	more	most
well	better	best

NOTE:

The adjective *good* and the adverb *well* may confuse a student. *Good* is always used as an adjective. *Well* is always used as an adverb.

Examples:

She is a good driver. (adjective)

She sings well. (adverb)

When referring to a person's health, the adverb *well* is always used.

Example:

Tom's throat hurts. He does not feel well.

Well is an adverb referring to Tom's health.

Spelling Tips

A. To form the comparative of adjectives or adverbs that end in "y," change the "y" to "i" and add "er" to the end of the word.

Example:

happy + er = happier

B. To form the superlative of adjectives or adverbs that end in "y," change the "y" to "i" and add "est" to the end of the word.

Example:

happy + est = happiest

EXERCISE E: Write the comparative and superlative forms of the following words. The first one has been done as an example for you.

		Comparative	**Superlative**
1.	modern	more modern	most modern
2.	great		
3.	easy		
4.	near		
5.	sad		
6.	scary		
7.	thin		
8.	loud		

EXERCISE F: Complete the following sentences using the comparative form of the word in parentheses. The first one has been done as an example for you.

1. This summer is rainy. However, last summer was <u>rainier</u> (rainy).

2. It is not very windy today. It was _____ (windy) yesterday.

3.   She is very polite. I am _____ (polite).

4.   My dog is pretty. Your dog is _____ (pretty).

5.   New York is beautiful. However, some people think San Francisco is _____ (beautiful).

EXERCISE G: Complete the following sentences by using the superlative form of the word in parentheses. The first one has been done as an example for you.

1.   Susan is the <u>oldest</u> (old) of the three sisters.

2.   He is the _____ (funny) person I know.

3.   Hong Wu is the _____ (good) best player on the basketball team.

4.   That is the _____ (bad) chocolate ice cream I have ever tasted.

5.   My final paper in history was my _____ (good) this semester.

See Appendices L and M for more information.

MODIFICATION—GRAMMAR

ANSWER KEY

Exercise A:

1. a	2. an	3. an	4. a
5. a	6. a	7. an	8. an

Exercise B:

1. the	2. the	3. a, the	4. the, the
5. an, the	6. the	7. the, a, a	

Exercise C:

1. These	2. this	3. those
4. that	5. these	6. this

Exercise D:

1. delicious	2. strict	3. careful
4. well	5. beautifully	

Exercise E:

	Comparative	Superlative
1.	more modern	most modern
2.	greater	greatest
3.	easier	easiest
4.	nearer	nearest
5.	sadder	saddest
6.	scarier	scariest
7.	thinner	thinnest
8.	louder	loudest

Exercise F:

1. rainier	2. windier	3. more polite
4. prettier	5. more beautiful	

Exercise G:

1. oldest	2. funniest	3. best
4. worst	5. best	

VISUALIZING PICTURES

A Living Room

The woman reads in her living room.

1. ceiling
2. wall
3. floor
4. curtains
5. chair

6. lamp
7. phone
8. end table
9. coffee table
10. rug

11. sofa
12. bookshelf
13. stereo
14. television

EXERCISE A: Change the following adjectives to adverbs. The first one has been done as an example for you.

	Adjectives		Adverbs
1.	neat	1.	neatly
2.	comfortable	2.	_____
3.	plain	3.	_____
4.	pretty	4.	_____
5.	clean	5.	_____

EXERCISE B: Compare ten objects in your living room to the ones labeled in the picture. Use comparative and superlative forms. The first one has been done as an example for you.

1. The sofa in my living room is bigger than the sofa in the picture.

2. _____

_____

3. _____

_____

4. _____

_____

5. _____

_____

6. _____

_____

7. _____

_____

8. _____

_____

9. _____

_____

10. _____

_____

Man Making Bed

The man makes his bed.

1.	closet	6.	floor	11.	sheet
2.	dresser	7.	bed	12.	mattress
3.	drawer	8.	pillow	13.	alarm clock
4.	air conditioner	9.	pillowcase	14.	bedstand
5.	curtains	10.	blanket		

EXERCISE A: List ten things you see in the picture. Use an adjective and an article with exercise items one through five and an article only with items six through ten. The first one has been done as an example for you.

1. a short man _____

2. _____

3. _____

4. _____

5. _____

6. _____

7. _____

8. _____

9. _____

10. _____

EXERCISE B: Complete the following sentences using *a*, *an*, or *the*. The first one has been done as an example for you.

1. The suits are in the closet.

2. _____ carpet is pretty.

3. Did you know there was _____ air conditioner in the room?

4. _____ room needs some more pictures.

5. _____ small rug near _____ bed would be nice also.

6. Is there _____ pillow on the bed?

7. _____ picture near the window is pretty.

8. _____ curtains match _____ bedspread.

9. _____ alarm clock can be very useful.

10. _____ night table has two drawers.

EXERCISE C: Complete the following sentences using the superlative or comparative form. The first one has been done as an example for you.

1. The bed is <u>bigger</u> than my bed.

2. The man is _____ than I.

3. The dresser is _____ than the night table.

4. The picture is the _____ I have ever seen.

5. The room is _____ than my room.

At a Restaurant

The restaurant is very busy.

1. chef
2. chef's assistant
3. booth
4. water glass

5. waiter
6. busboy
7. waitress
8. menu

9. chair
10. smoking section
11. no smoking section
12. hostess

*Many U.S. and Canadian restaurants do not allow smoking at all.

EXERCISE A: Look at the picture and decide whether the following statements are true or false by writing T (true) or F (false) in the blank provided. The first one has been done as an example for you.

___F___   1. The people in the picture are at a party.

_____   2. All of the people in the picture know each other.

_____   3. The restaurant has booths.

_____   4. The restaurant is probably not very expensive.

_____   5. The people in the restaurant are having a horrible time.

EXERCISE B: Use *a, an,* or *the* to complete the following sentences. Use the correct article to fill in the blank. The first one has been done as an example for you.

1. The woman on the telephone is standing behind the counter.

2. _____ busboy is pouring water into the glass.

3. There is _____ family waiting to be seated.

4. There is _____ empty table.

5. _____ waiter is standing behind _____ chair.

EXERCISE C: Use the comparative or superlative forms to complete the following sentences. The first one has been done as an example for you.

1. These hamburgers are bigger than yours, Mom.

2. This restaurant is _____ than the one we went to last week.

3. This restaurant closes _____ than the one next door.

4. The seats are _____ than the one we ate at yesterday.

5. The waiters are _____ than the ones at "Happy Eating" family restaurant.

Street Traffic

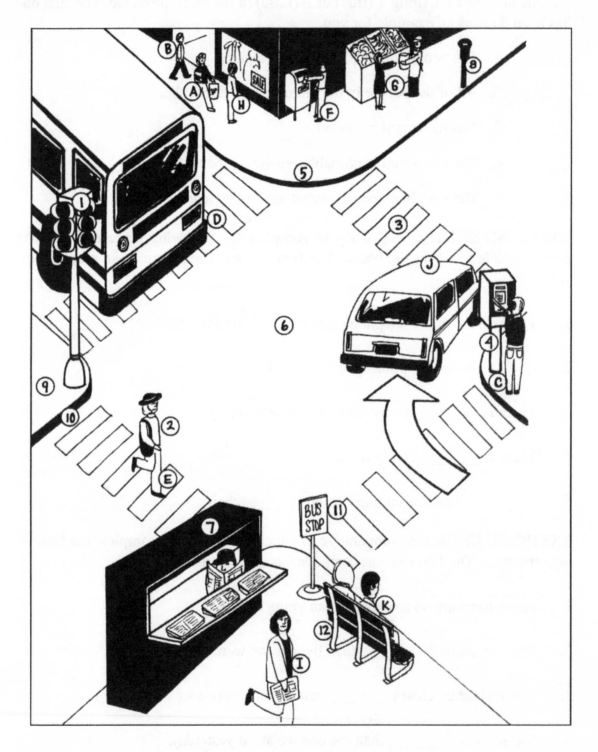

There is a lot of traffic at the intersection.

EXERCISE A: Look at the picture and write true or false to the following sentences by writing T (true) or F (false) in the blank provided. The first one has been done as an example for you.

____T____ 1. It could be about 9:00 in the morning.

_____ 2. There are four people at the bus stop.

_____ 3. The newsstand is closed.

_____ 4. The bus is probably very late.

_____ 5. Someone is receiving a letter.

EXERCISE B: Write ten sentences describing what you see in the picture. The adjectives, adverbs, nouns, articles, phrases, and verbs listed below are suggestions for your sentences. The first one has been done as an example for you.

1.	traffic light	A.	come out of the store
2.	pedestrian	B.	go into the store
3.	crosswalk	C.	make a phone call
4.	public telephone	D.	Stop
5.	corner	E.	cross the street
6.	intersection	F.	mail a letter
7.	newsstand	G.	buy groceries
8.	parking meter	H.	look at the windows/clothes
9.	sidewalk	I.	walk
10.	curb	J.	turn
11.	bus stop	K.	wait for the bus
12.	bench		

1. A man is walking into the store. _____

_____

2. _____

_____

3. _____

_____

4. _____

_____

5. _____

_____

6. _____

_____

7. _____

_____

8. _____

_____

9. _____

_____

10. _____

_____

MODIFICATION—VISUALIZING PICTURES

ANSWER KEY

A Living Room
Exercise A:

Adjective	Adverb
1. neat	neatly
2. comfortable	comfortably
3. plain	plainly
4. pretty	prettily
5. clean	cleanly

Exercise B:

Answers will vary.
Here are some examples:
1. The sofa in my living room is bigger than the sofa in the picture.
2. My coffee table has more books on it than the table in the picture.
3. The room in the picture has only one window with curtains while mine has three.
4. There is a bookshelf in the picture but none in my living room.
5. I don't have a stereo in my living room like the one in the picture.
6. The lamp in my living room stands on the floor unlike the lamp in the picture.
7. My living room has wood floors, not a rug like the one in the picture.
8. The room in the picture has only one chair, my living room has two.
9. My living room is much smaller than the one shown.
10. My living room in the picture is much neater than mine.

Man Making Bed
Exercise A:

1. a short man
2. a big bed
3. a small night table
4. a plain floor
5. a neat room
6. a lamp
7. a pillow

8. a suit
9. a pair of shoes
10. a picture

Note: You may have used different adjectives and articles from the ones listed.

Exercise B:

1. The, the	2. The	3. an	4. The
5. A, the	6. a	7. The	8. The, the
9. An	10. The		

Exercise C:

Answers will vary.
Here are some examples:

1. bigger	4. prettiest
2. taller	5. larger
3. wider	

At a Restaurant

Exercise A:

1. F	2. F	3. T
4. T	5. F	

Exercise B:

1. The	2. The	3. a
4. an	5. The, a	

Exercise C:

Answers will vary.
Here are some examples:

1. bigger	4. more comfortable
2. better	5. quicker
3. earlier	

Street Traffic

Exercise A:

1. T	2. F	3. F
4. F	5. F	

Exercise B:

Answers will vary.

Here are some examples:

1. A man is walking into the store.
2. A woman wearing a hat is crossing the street.
3. A car is turning right at the intersection.
4. Someone has stopped on the sidewalk to look at the clothes in the window.
5. A man has stopped at the public telephone to make a phone call.
6. The woman has stopped to buy groceries at the stand.
7. The bus has come to a stop at the intersection.
8. The newsstand sells newspapers and magazines.
9. A woman has gone to the mailbox to mail a letter.
10. The person with the shopping bag has just come out of the store.

READING

Topic 1: The Public Library

Vocabulary

department—a part of something

elderly—a person who is old

fiction—a story that is not true

job listing—information about a job

library—a collection of books, newspapers, and magazines on many subjects

nonfiction—a true story

search—to look for something

A library contains information on many subjects, like how to plant a vegetable garden or how to prepare an American-food dish. The library serves the area where it is located.

The library is divided into departments. The administrative department is made up of the head librarian, who runs the daily operations of the library, and the building manager, who makes sure the building's lighting, heating, and air conditioning systems are working. The technical services department orders books and catalogs them. The general information department contains fiction and nonfiction books on many subjects. This department also has dictionaries, maps, telephone directories, newspapers, and magazines. The business reference department contains information on area businesses. There is also a children's department, which contains fiction and nonfiction books for children, and an audiovisual department that has films and CDs. People can check out books, films, and CDs.

A library offers special programs to the community. For example, the children's department offers story hours for toddlers and summer reading programs for children. The general information department takes books to people who are sick, elderly, or disabled and who cannot come to the library. The business reference department helps people search for jobs by having job listings.

A library is very important to the community that it serves. It can provide the answer to any question.

EXERCISE A: Answer the following questions on the lines provided.

1. List the departments in a library.

    _____

    _____

    _____

2. What does the head librarian do?

    _____

    _____

    _____

3. What types of programs does the children's department offer?

    _____

    _____

    _____

4. What services does the general information department offer to the community?

    _____

    _____

    _____

EXERCISE B: Underline the adjectives in the following sentences from the passage. The first one has been done for you as an example.

1. A library contains information on <u>many</u> subjects.

2. A library contains information on how to prepare American food.

3. The building manager makes sure the air conditioning system is working.

4. The business reference department contains information on area businesses.

5. A library offers special programs to the community.

Discussion:

How do libraries in America differ from libraries in your native country? The instructor may wish to invite a librarian from the local public library to speak to the class about the services the library offers to the community.

Topic 2: Fire Safety

Vocabulary

designated—something specific

kitchen—the room where food is cooked

smoke detector—a device that can sense smoke

space heater—a device used to heat rooms

Flames raged through the home at 307 Oakdale Road this morning killing a mother and her son, age three, as they slept.

According to fire chief Steven Blair, "A pile of trash was sitting next to a space heater. The heat sparked a fire, and the fire quickly spread through the house. The home did not have a smoke detector."

Chief Blair is using the fire as a plea to people to make their homes safe from fire. First, every home or apartment should have at least one smoke detector that works. The detector should be checked every thirty days to make sure it is working properly. The batteries should be replaced every six months, and the detector changed every ten years. Second, do not leave trash next to a furnace or heater. Trash can burn in only a few minutes. Third, many fires originate in the kitchen. A person should never leave the kitchen while food is cooking. Fourth, never let children play with matches. Finally, create a fire escape plan. If your house has more than one floor or if you live on the upper floor in an apartment building, make sure you have a safe way to get to the ground. Once out, your family should have a designated place to meet.

Practice your escape plan every month.

"A home safety plan is very important," said Chief Blair. "It can save your life, your child's life, and your pet's life."

For additional information on home fire safety, contact the fire department educator at (336) 555-0102.

EXERCISE A: Answer the following questions on the lines below.

1. Write the route to the nearest fire exit in your school building. (Hint: The fire escape route should be posted on the wall of your classroom.)

    _____

    _____

    _____

2. What caused the fire at 307 Oakdale?

    _____

    _____

    _____

3. How should a smoke detector be maintained?

_____

_____

_____

4. How should fire safety be handled in the kitchen?

_____

_____

_____

5. Explain why a home fire escape plan is important.

_____

_____

_____

EXERCISE B: Change the following adjectives from the passage into adverbs. The first one has been done as an example for you.

	Adjective	Adverb
1.	quick	quickly
2.	proper	_____
3.	final	_____
4.	important	_____
5.	safe	_____

Discussion:

Have students discuss ways fire safety can be improved in their homes. Students may wish to create a list of fire safety tips to post in their homes and develop a fire escape plan. The instructor may wish to invite the fire department educator to speak to the class about fire safety.

Topic 3: Childproofing Your Home

Vocabulary

childproofing—make a home safe for a child

medicine cabinet—a place where medicine is stored

safety gate—a gate that prevents a child from falling down the stairs

A safe home is important to every parent. Before a child is born, the parent should get down on the floor and see the home from a child's eye level. Notice how easily the cabinets can be reached or how easily the child can get into the bathroom without being noticed.

The kitchen should be childproofed. Install locks on the cabinets, so a child cannot swallow household cleansers. Remove knobs from stove burners and ovens, so a child cannot turn them on. Place a wedge under a stove and refrigerator so that they will not tilt over on a child.

The bathroom is another room that should be childproofed. A child should never be left alone in the bathroom. A child could accidentally turn on the hot water in the sink or bathtub and be burned. Or a child could fall into the bathtub. A child can drown in one inch of water. A lock should be placed on the medicine cabinet. Medicine should be kept out of a child's reach.

Front and back doors should also be childproofed. Once a child is tall enough to reach the door knob, he or she can leave the house without a parent's knowledge. An additional chain lock should be placed at the top of the door to prevent the child from getting out.

Stairways are another concern. A safety gate should be installed at the top and bottom of stairways. This will prevent a child from falling down the stairs.

As a child grows, change your child proofing. For example, if a child can unlock one style of lock, change the lock to one a child cannot unlock. Childproofing a home will keep your child safe and prevent an accident.

EXERCISE A: Answer the following questions on the lines below.

1. Why is childproofing a home important?

    _____

    _____

    _____

2. Explain the importance of childproofing a kitchen.

    _____

    _____

    _____

3. Why does a bathroom pose a hazard to a child?

    _____

    _____

    _____

4. Why is a safety gate important?

    _____

    _____

    _____

EXERCISE B: Underline the adjectives and adverbs in the following sentences from the passage. The first one has been done as an example for you.

1. Install locks on the cabinets, so a child cannot swallow <u>household</u> cleansers.

2.   A child could accidentally turn on the hot water in the sink or bathtub.

3.   A lock should be placed on the medicine cabinet.

4.   A safety gate should be installed at the top and bottom of stairways.

5.   Childproofing a home will keep your child safe.

Discussion:

Are homes in your native country childproof? If so, explain the safety precautions parents take. The instructor may wish to invite a nurse from a pediatrician's office to explain childproofing a home.

Topic 4: Weekend Activities

Vocabulary

miniature—small

museum—a place where old things are kept

park—a grassy place that has swings and picnic tables

stable—a building where a horse lives

Are you bored? Do you need an activity to fill your free time? If so, look to the city where you live. American cities offer many exciting activities.

There are parks where people can go. The parks have picnic areas and rides for children. For example, in High Point, North Carolina, each neighborhood has its own park for children. All the equipment is handicapped accessible. Children can swing or play on a fort with slides and ladders. In addition to neighborhood parks, there is City Lake Park and Oak Hollow Lake. City Lake Park has a swimming pool, a miniature train, and a 1930s fire truck for children to climb onto. There are also picnic tables, picnic shelters, and fishing. Oak Hollow Lake also offers picnic tables, picnic shelters, and fishing. Oak Hollow has other fun activities such as boating, tennis facilities, a golf course, and a campground.

People can also take advantage of nature trails for bicycle riding and running. There also may be stables with horses for riding.

People can also visit the city's historical museum. This type of museum preserves the city's history. The Greensboro Historical Museum in Greensboro, North Carolina, has exhibits about two famous residents: Dolly Madison, a wife of a former United States president, and William Sidney Porter, a writer, known to Americans as O. Henry.

Call your Chamber of Commerce or library for a list of activities in your area. You will never be bored again.

EXERCISE A: Answer the following questions on the lines below.

1. Name some activities you can do in your town.

    _____

    _____

    _____

2. What are the differences between City Lake Park and Oak Hollow Lake?

    _____

    _____

    _____

3. What is an historical museum?

    _____

    _____

    _____

4. Where can you find information about activities in your area?

    _____

    _____

    _____

EXERCISE B: Underline the adjectives in the following sentences from the passage. The first one has been done as an example for you.

1. American cities offer many exciting activities.

2. City Lake Park has a miniature train.

3. They can also visit the city's historical museum.

4. The museum has exhibits about two famous residents.

5. Dolly Madison was the wife of a former United States president.

Discussion:

Discuss places you have visited in your city. The instructor may wish to invite someone from the city's Public Information Office to discuss activities the town has to offer its residents.

MODIFICATION—READING

ANSWER KEY

Topic 1
Exercise A:

1. The departments in a library are administrative, technical services, general information, business reference, children's, and audiovisual.
2. The head librarian runs the daily operations of a library.
3. The children's department offers story hours for toddlers and summer reading programs.
4. The general information department takes books to people who are sick, elderly, or disabled and who cannot come to the library.

Exercise B:

1. many
2. American-food
3. building, air conditioning
4. business reference, area
5. special

Topic 2
Exercise A:

1. Answers will vary. Example: Turn left at classroom. Take second right down the stairs and out the doors.
2. The fire was caused by trash sitting next to a space heater.
3. The smoke detector should be checked every thirty days, batteries replaced every six months, and the detector should be changed every ten years.
4. A person should never leave the kitchen while food is cooking.
5. A home fire escape plan helps people get out of their home safely in the event of a fire.

Exercise B:

1. quickly
2. properly
3. finally
4. more important
5. safely

Topic 3

Exercise A:

1. Childproofing a home can save a child's life.
2. The kitchen should be childproofed, so a child cannot swallow household cleansers or turn on the stove.
3. The bathroom poses a hazard to a child because a child could be burned by hot water or drown in the bathtub.
4. A safety gate prevents a child from falling down the stairs.

Exercise B:

1. household
2. accidentally, hot
3. medicine
4. safety
5. Childproofing

Topic 4

Exercise A:

1. Answers will vary. Example: Our town has a swimming pool, hiking trails, and a zoo.
2. City Lake Park has a swimming pool, a miniature train, and a 1930s fire truck. Oak Hollow Lake has boating, tennis facilities, a golf course, and a campground.
3. An historical museum preserves a city's history.
4. Answers will vary. Example: The two best places to get information about activities in my town are the Department of Parks and Recreation and the Chamber of Tourism and Commerce.

Exercise B:

1. American, many, exciting
2. miniature
3. city's, historical
4. two, famous
5. former, United States

LISTENING

Topic 1: Visiting a Friend

Vocabulary

agenda—plan

escalator—a moving staircase

exhibit—a show; for example, an art show

tour—a trip for pleasure, business, or education, normally involving a series of stops that end up at the starting point

Jack is coming to visit his friend Susan, who lives in New York City, for a week. Listen to your teacher or partner read their conversation:

SUSAN: I still can't believe you're finally coming. We'll have an incredible time.

JACK: I'm really looking forward to it. What's our agenda?

SUSAN: Well, your flight arrives at 6:30 in the evening. We could have dinner at this great little restaurant in my neighborhood. Then, depending on how you feel, we could have a quick tour of my neighborhood.

JACK: That sounds great. What other items do you have planned for the rest of the week?

SUSAN: Well, we can go to the Museum of Modern Art. There's an exhibit by Picasso.

JACK: Oh, he's one of my favorite painters. I'm really interested in his work.

SUSAN: On another evening, we can go to this beautiful restaurant by the sea. It's very quiet and peaceful. I'm sure you'll love it.

JACK: Susie, I'm sorry about causing you so much trouble. Is New York very different from Toronto?

SUSAN: Yes. It's much noisier and much more crowded. The streets are dirtier too. But it's much more exciting and less expensive. You can't be bored here. It's like having six or seven different countries in one place.

JACK: Well, I'll see for myself tomorrow. I just looked at my watch, and I'd better go.

SUSAN: Okay. Remember, I'll be standing by the ticket counter next to the escalators.

JACK: Thanks again. See you tomorrow.

EXERCISE A: Answer true or false to the following statements by writing T (true) or F (false) in the blank provided. The first one has been done as an example for you.

___F___ 1. Jack lives in New York City.

_____ 2. They are both from Toronto.

_____ 3. Jack's flight arrives at 6:30 in the morning.

_____ 4. Jack does not like Picasso.

_____ 5. Susan thinks New York is more exciting than Toronto.

_____ 6. Susan will not meet Jack at the airport tomorrow.

_____ 7. Susan and Jack are both looking forward to seeing each other.

_____ 8. Susan has recently visited six different countries.

EXERCISE B: Complete the following sentences using *a*, *an*, or *the*. The first one has been done as an example for you.

1. We'll have <u>a</u> great week.

2. Your flight arrived _____ hour earlier.

3. We could have _____ good dinner.

4. There's _____ exhibit by Picasso at _____ Museum of Modern Art.

5. I just read _____ book on history, my favorite subject.

6. There's _____ restaurant by the sea.

EXERCISE C: Underline the adjectives in the following sentences from the passage. The first one has been done as an example for you.

1. We'll have an <u>incredible</u> time.

2. We could have dinner at this great little restaurant in my neighborhood.

3. He's one of my favorite painters.

4. We could go to this beautiful restaurant by the sea.

5. It's like having six or seven countries in one place.

Discussion

Describe a place you have been to in America that you really liked. Use as many adjectives and adverbs as you can. Compare this place to a similar type of place in your native country using comparative forms (more exciting, less expensive, bigger, etc.). Write your answer on the lines below. Then, share your answers with the class.

_____

_____

_____

_____

_____

_____

_____

_____

_____

Topic 2: Getting Ready to Leave

Vocabulary

destination—the end of a trip, the place where you want to go

heavy—weighing a lot

host—someone who has a party or dinner to which you are invited

misplace—cannot find

scenery—view

various—some

Listen as your teacher or partner reads the following conversation between George and Janet and look at the pictures.

JANET: George, hurry up. It's 7:00 in the evening, and we have to be there at 8:30. Traffic could be heavy.

GEORGE: Wait, I can't find my tie.

JANET: Wear the red one. It's in the closet next to your gray suit. I put it there this morning.

GEORGE: Where are my keys? They're not in my pocket.

JANET: Maybe they're on the table in the kitchen. Yes, here they are.

GEORGE: Have you seen my black shoes?

JANET: Yes, they're by the door in the living room. Oh, no. I can't find my earrings.

GEORGE: Aren't they on the dresser in your jewelry case?

JANET: I looked, but they weren't there. Oh, I think they're in my coat pocket. No, they're not there.

GEORGE: Oh, here they are.

JANET: Thank you. Where were they?

GEORGE: Under the kitchen table. The cat was sitting on them.

JANET: Okay, we have everything. Are we ready to leave?

GEORGE: Yes. Do you have the directions?

JANET: Yes, it's on Pickston Street and Bower Avenue next to the movie theater and opposite the Savoy Hotel.

GEORGE: I know where that is. We had a conference at the Savoy once.

EXERCISE A: On the pictures shown, label each of the items that are misplaced in the order you hear them. You can put 1, 2, 3, etc. next to the pictures of the missing items.

EXERCISE B: Answer true or false to the following questions by writing T (true) or F (false) in the blank provided. The first one has been done as an example for you.

__F__   1. George and Janet need to leave the house by 6:00.

_____   2. The couple have misplaced various things.

_____   3. George and Janet have no pets.

_____   4. The couple are going to the Savoy Hotel for a conference.

_____   5. The couple cannot go out tonight because they lost their keys.

EXERCISE C: Listen as your teacher or partner re-reads the following sentences as Janet and George talk about their night on the way home. Choose the correct word to complete the sentences. The first one has been done as an example for you.

1. Don't drive too (quick, <u>quickly</u>) or else we'll miss our turn.

2. Everyone was very (friend, friendly), didn't you think?

3. Oh yes, and the food was (excellent, excellently), especially the seafood.

4. Didn't you think it was a bit (noisy, noisily) though? Especially Bob, he speaks very (loud, loudly).

5. What did you think of the singer? I thought she was very (beautiful, beautifully) and sang very (good, well).

6. Oh, but poor Bill, dropping his glasses. He should be more (careful, carefully).

7. The scenery was (lovely, beautifully) though. It would have been better if it weren't raining very (heavy, heavily).

8. I agree. Oh, it was very (nice, nicely) to see Sue after many years. She was always such a (quiet, quietly) person.

9. Well, I think, overall, we had a (wonderful, wonderfully) time. Next time we'll get there (early, earlier).

10. I agree. I'm (tired, tiredly) though. Tonight, I'm sure I'll have a (good, well) night's sleep.

Discussion

Did you attend a party or any other social event since coming to America? Where was it? Describe it. Was it very different from a similar type of event in your own native country? Discuss some of the differences in social etiquette between the two countries. For example, do you need to take a gift to your host's house? What are some acceptable gifts? In America, most people arrive 15 to 20 minutes after the appointed time for parties. Is it the same or different in your country?

Topic 3: Jamaican Vacation

Vocabulary

bartender—someone who makes the drinks in a bar

local—belonging to a certain place, not from another country

memorable—something you will remember for a long time

Map of Where Ann and Bob Are Staying

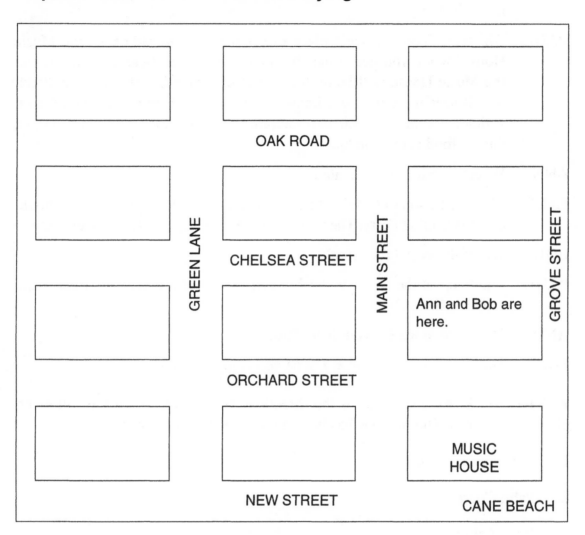

OAK ROAD

GREEN LANE

CHELSEA STREET

MAIN STREET

GROVE STREET

Ann and Bob are here.

ORCHARD STREET

MUSIC HOUSE

NEW STREET

CANE BEACH

Ann and her husband, Bob, are on vacation in Jamaica. Listen as your teacher or partner reads their conversation asking a local bartender (Paul) for directions to the best places to see.

PAUL: So, how are you enjoying your stay here?

ANN: Oh, it's a beautiful country. I love the hot, sunny weather, and the beaches are so clean and pretty.

PAUL: What about you, Bob?

BOB: Oh, it's perfect, very relaxing, and yet it's so busy. There are always lots of people on the beach and streets.

ANN: Anyway, we were wondering if you could tell us what are the best places to see in Kingston?

PAUL: Oh, sure. There's a great place to listen to live music called the Music House. When you get to the sign that says, "Cane Beach," turn left and the Music House will be on the corner of Grove Street and New Street. You'll hear the music and know you're there. There's also Palm Court, which is the most delicious restaurant in this area. It's small and simple, but the food is memorable.

ANN: Where is Palm Court located?

PAUL: It's on the corner of Main and New Street on the left. Oh, and you should take the Capital Ferry. The view is wonderful, especially in the evening.

BOB: Where do we get the ferry?

PAUL: Right across the street at the Boat Station on the corner of Green Lane and New Street.

ANN: Thanks so much for your help, Paul.

PAUL: You're welcome, anytime. I hope you enjoy Jamaica.

EXERCISE A: As you listen to the directions from Paul, locate the following places on the map. The first one has been done as an example for you.

1. The Music House

2. Palm Court

3. Boat Station

EXERCISE B: Now listen as your teacher or partner reads the dialogue again and answer true or false to the following by writing T (true) or F (false) in the blank provided. The first one has been done as an example for you.

___F___ 1. The bartender's name is Bob.

_____ 2. Palm Court is a beautiful garden.

_____ 3. The couple thinks Jamaica is very beautiful.

_____ 4. Paul does not think they should go on the ferry.

EXERCISE C: Complete the following sentences using *a*, *an*, or *the*. The first one has been done as an example for you.

1. Was <u>the</u> ferry ride wonderful?

2. There is _____ delicious restaurant in this area. It is _____ best for seafood.

3. _____ food in _____ restaurant across _____ street is also very good.

4. Kingston is _____ capital of Jamaica.

5. Paul: What do you think of Jamaica?
    Ann: Oh, it's _____ beautiful country. It has _____ most delicious seafood.

Discussion

Have you ever been a tourist in another country? Describe your experience. Do you sometimes feel like a tourist in America? Explain and give examples.

Topic 4: Ordering Takeout Dinner

Vocabulary

address—the street where a person lives (an address contains a house or apartment number, street name, city, and state)

dinner—the last meal of the day (in America, a person eats three meals a day: breakfast in the morning, lunch at midday, and dinner in the evening)

Listen as your teacher or partner reads the following conversation of Dawn ordering dinner for herself and her husband on the telephone.

WAITER: Hello. Great Wall Restaurant. May I help you?

DAWN: Yes. I'd like to order dinner please, delivery.

WAITER: What's your address?

DAWN: 416 Woodrow Street, apartment #2. We're the third house on the right.

WAITER: Which streets is it between?

DAWN: It's between Carlson and Raven Streets.

WAITER: What would you like?

DAWN: I'd like hot and sour soup and cold sesame noodles. Also, I'd like hot and spicy chicken with peppers and sweet and sour chicken.

WAITER: Do you want white rice or brown?

DAWN: White, please.

WAITER: Okay, I'll see you in 25 minutes. That'll be $8.25.

DAWN: Okay. Great.

EXERCISE A: Now listen as your teacher or partner reads the dialogue again and answer true or false to the following questions by writing T (true) or F (false) in the blank provided. The first one has been done as an example for you.

___T___   1. The restaurant is a Chinese restaurant.

_____   2. Dawn is probably going to spend the evening at home with her husband.

_____   3. The time now is 8:25.

_____   4. Dawn lives between Carlson and Woodrow Streets.

_____   5. Dawn decided to order an appetizer.

_____   6. Dawn and her husband do not like spicy food.

EXERCISE B: List five food items that were mentioned in the conversation between Dawn and the waiter on the lines below. The first one has been done as an example for you.

1. hot and sour soup _____

2. _____

3. _____

4. _____

5. _____

Discussion

Do restaurants in your native country deliver food to homes? What do you think of this idea?

MODIFICATION—LISTENING

ANSWER KEY

Topic 1: Visiting a Friend

Exercise A:

1. F
2. F
3. F (Jack's flight arrives 6:30 in the evening)
4. F
5. T
6. F
7. T
8. F (Susan describes New York City as "having six or seven countries in one place".)

Exercise B:

1. a	2. an	3. a
4. an, the	5. a	6. a

Exercise C

1. incredible
2. great, little
3. favorite
4. this, beautiful
5. six, seven, one

Topic 2: Getting Ready to Leave

Exercise A:

In the order in which items are listed.
1. tie
2. keys
3. shoes
4. earrings

Exercise B:

1. F
2. T

3. F
4. F (George was at a conference at the Savoy Hotel once, but that is not the reason they are going tonight.)
5. F (George found their keys.)

Exercise C:

1. quickly
2. friendly
3. excellent
4. noisy, loudly
5. beautiful, well
6. careful
7. lovely, heavily
8. nice, quiet
9. wonderful, earlier
10. tired, good

Topic 3: Jamaican Vacation

Exercise A

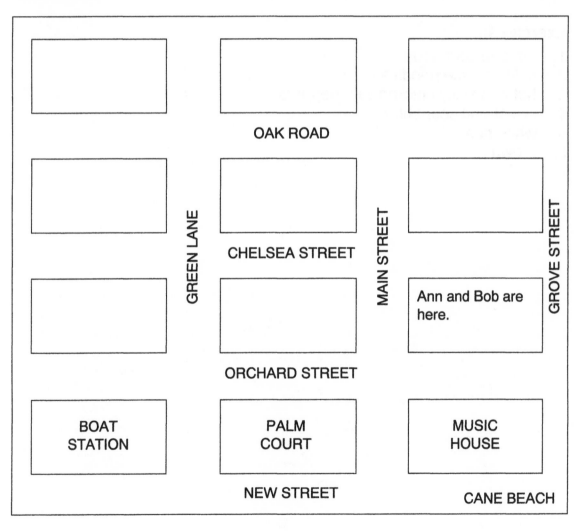

Exercise B:

1. F (It is Paul)
2. F (It is a restaurant)
3. T
4. F

Exercise C:

1. the
2. a, the
3. The, the, the
4. the
5. a, the

Topic 4: Ordering Dinner

Exercise A:

1. T
2. T
3. F
4. F
5. F
6. F

Exercise B:

1. hot and sour soup
2. cold sesame noodles
3. hot and spicy chicken with peppers
4. sweet and sour chicken
5. white rice
6. brown rice

ACTIVITIES

Activity 1: Restaurant

Vocabulary

aim—what you want to accomplish, your goal

competitors—people or groups that are trying to get the same thing that you want

compiled—put together

fed up—tired

greasy—too much oil

profit—the money you make after expenses

promotion—offer that gives something at a cheaper price or for free

You and your friends are fed up with the terrible food that is being served in your neighborhood. The burgers and chicken are greasy. It is too expensive, and the restaurant seats are too small and very uncomfortable.

Together you and your friends have saved the money, and you are ready to make a plan for your restaurant and its menu.

You aim to:

a. please your customers

b. serve delicious but inexpensive food

c. make a profit

NOTE: An actual plan should be drawn and a list and description of dishes compiled.

Describe the exact amount and location of the following things.

1. Tables. How many? Where?

    _____

    _____

2. Chairs. How many? Where?

    _____

    _____

3. Bathroom(s). Location? Number?

    _____

    _____

4. Kitchen. Location?

    _____

    _____

5. Storage room. Where?

    _____

    _____

6. Cash register. Location?

    _____

    _____

7. The dessert showcase. Location? Number?

_____

_____

8. Pictures. Location? Number?

_____

_____

Use ten adjectives to describe what you would like your restaurant to look and feel like. Include the colors of the furniture, the size of things, etc.

1. _____

2. _____

3. _____

4. _____

5. _____

6. _____

7. _____

8. _____

9. _____

10. _____

List ten different foods, including three desserts, that you would like to serve in the restaurant. You can use your favorites from your own native country. Use adjectives to describe each one, for example, spicy. Finally, include the recipes.

1. Dish and description: _____

   _____

   Recipe: _____

   _____

   _____

2. Dish and description: _____

   _____

   Recipe: _____

   _____

   _____

3. Dish and description: _____

   _____

   Recipe: _____

   _____

   _____

4. Dish and description: _____

   _____

   Recipe: _____

   _____

   _____

5. Dish and description: _____

_____

Recipe: _____

_____

_____

6. Dish and description: _____

_____

Recipe: _____

_____

_____

7. Dish and description: _____

_____

Recipe: _____

_____

_____

8. Dish and description: _____

_____

Recipe: _____

_____

_____

9. Dish and description: _____

    _____

    Recipe: _____

    _____

    _____

10. Dish and description: _____

    _____

    Recipe: _____

    _____

    _____

List five different promotions that could help improve business. The first one has been done as an example for you.

1. Give free desserts to anyone who orders food in the value of $20 or more.

    _____

2. _____

    _____

3. _____

    _____

4. _____

    _____

5. _____

    _____

Discussion

Have you been to a restaurant in the United States that prepares food from your native country? Describe it to the class. Did you like it? Why, or why not? Do you miss your native country's food? Explain.

Activity 2: Personal Ad

Vocabulary

companionship—a relationship in which people frequently spend time together

diplomatic—polite, not saying what you really feel if it offends someone else

energetic—having a lot of energy

enthusiastic—excited

flexible—being open-minded, able to change

generous—someone who likes to give

perceptive—being able to understand another person's feelings or thoughts

spontaneous—not planning things, just doing them

Writing Your Own Personal Ad

Example:

I am 6' 1" and described as handsome, creative, intelligent, sensitive, cheerful, and loyal. I am a hardworking, successful lawyer looking for someone similar to myself (occupation not important) to have interesting conversations with, take long walks with, to share a beautiful companionship. For more information contact P.O. Box 5574.

List five adjectives the writer uses to describe himself. The first one has been done as an example for you.

1. handsome _____

2. _____

3. _____

4. _____

5. _____

Without repeating any of the adjectives the writer used, list five adjectives describing the person he is seeking. The first one has been done as an example for you.

1. caring _____

2. _____

3. _____

4. _____

5. _____

Choose five adjectives from the list below to describe yourself and five to describe the person you are seeking.

artistic	loyal	witty	beautiful	enthusiastic
generous	gentle	easygoing	polite	funny
happy	perceptive	friendly	honest	kind
flexible	diplomatic	intelligent	interesting	careful
energetic	spontaneous	handsome	tall	short
pretty	sad	shy	outgoing	young
old				

Write your own personal ad using the personal ad given as an example. Exchange it with your partner. You and your partner should then go over each other's lists and add adjectives you would use to describe your partner. Go over the new lists together.

After your ads are finished, type them up, and place a small photo of yourselves at the top.

Discussion

Are personal ads used to find partners in your native country? What do you think of them? Do you think they are a good way of finding a partner? Explain your answer. Would you ever place a personal ad in a newspaper? Why or why not?

REVIEW

Key Points

1. An adjective refers to a person, a pronoun, or any other group of words playing the part of the noun.

2. An article is a type of adjective.

3. There are two types of articles—definite and indefinite.

4. A demonstrative pronoun is a type of adjective.

5. An adverb refers to a verb, an adjective, or another adverb.

6. The comparative form compares two persons, things, or groups.

7. The superlative form compares more than two persons, things, or groups.

EXERCISE A: Complete the following sentences by using *a*, *an*, or *the*. The first one has been done as an example for you.

1. A: Did you have a good time at <u>the</u> baseball game?
   B: Yes.
   C: I did too. Thanks for coming with me.

2. A: What did you do last night?

    B: I went to _____ party.

    A: Oh really. Whose party?

3. Do you have _____ money with you?

4. I had a small lunch, _____ apple, and _____ sandwich.

5. She is a student at _____ College of Music.

6. Trinidad is _____ island near South America.

EXERCISE B: Place *a, an,* or *the* where necessary in the following sentences. The first one has been done as an example for you.

1. Brazil is <u>the</u> biggest country in South America.

2. Yesterday I bought radio and TV. TV was expensive and radio did not work.

3. Man is on roof. What is he doing?

4. I think English is difficult language to learn, but it is most important language.

5. Look at flowers in garden. They are beautiful.

6. We had most delicious dinner at seafood restaurant.

7. End of movie was better than beginning.

8. I saw best movie at movie theater last night.

9. I read book on United States history that you told me about.

10. Do you have minute? I need to speak to you.

EXERCISE C: Underline the word that correctly completes the following sentences. The first one has been done as an example for you.

1. I closed the door (quiet, <u>quietly</u>) so that I would not disturb him.

2. His singing is (terrible, terribly).

3. Judy (hard, hardly) studied for her exam, so she did very (poor, poorly) on it.

4. He used to be my neighbor a long time ago, so I do not remember him very (good, well).

5. I am not very (good, well) at math.

EXERCISE D: Write the comparative form of the following words. The first one has been done as an example for you.

Comparative

1. good   better

2. cheap   _____

3. exciting   _____

4. intelligent   _____

5. interesting   _____

EXERCISE E: Complete the following sentences by writing the comparative form of the word in parentheses. The first one has been done as an example for you.

1. This restaurant is not expensive. It is _____ (expensive) than the other one.

2. This apple is sweet, but yours is _____ (sweet).

3. My garden hose is not very big. Yours is _____ (big).

4. Today is hot, but yesterday was _____ (hot).

5. The movie was not exciting. The one yesterday was _____ (exciting).

EXERCISE F: Write the superlative form of the following words. The first one has been done as an example for you.

Superlative

1. bad   worst
   _____

2. small
   _____

3. large
   _____

4. long
   _____

5. good
   _____

EXERCISE G: Complete the following sentences by writing the superlative form of the word in parentheses. The first one has been done as an example for you.

1. That is the <u>biggest</u> (big) watermelon I have seen in twenty years.

2. James is the _____ (small) boy in Mrs. Key's kindergarten class.

3. January 20 was the _____ (cold) day of the year.

4. Betty's Bridal Shop has the _____ (beautiful) wedding gowns in Lexington.

5. Sally said that her science paper was the _____ (difficult) paper she had ever written.

MODIFICATION—REVIEW

ANSWER KEY

Exercise A:

1. the
2. a
3. the
4. an, a
5. the
6. an

Exercise B:

1. Brazil is <u>the</u> biggest country in South America.

2. Yesterday I bought <u>a</u> radio and TV. <u>The</u> TV was expensive and <u>the</u> radio did not work.

3. <u>A</u> man is on <u>the</u> roof. What is he doing?

4. I think English is <u>a</u> difficult language to learn, but it is <u>the</u> most important language.

5. Look at <u>the</u> flowers in <u>the</u> garden. They are beautiful.

6. We had <u>the</u> most delicious dinner at <u>a</u> seafood restaurant.

7. <u>The</u> end of the movie was better than <u>the</u> beginning.

8. I saw <u>the</u> best movie at <u>the</u> movie theater last night.

9. I read <u>the</u> book on United States history that you told me about.

10. Do you have <u>a</u> minute? I need to speak to you.

Exercise C:

1. quietly
2. terrible
3. hardly, poorly
4. well
5. good

Exercise D:

1. better
2. cheaper
3. more exciting
4. more intelligent
5. more interesting

Exercise E:

1. more expensive
2. sweeter
3. bigger
4. hotter
5. more exciting

Exercise F:

1. worst
2. smallest
3. largest
4. longest
5. best

Exercise G:

1. biggest
2. smallest
3. coldest
4. most beautiful
5. most difficult

Appendix A

PARTS OF SPEECH

All words in a sentence have a particular function, and each is called a part of speech. In English there are eight parts of speech.

Noun—person, place or thing that performs the action

The **teacher** writes on the board.

Pronoun—word that takes the place of a noun and all of its modifiers

I am reading **a very interesting American history novel.** I am reading **it.**

Verb—word that shows action

The batter **hit** the ball and **scored** a home run.

Adjective—word that describes a noun or pronoun, including *a, an, the*

The beautiful garden has **many different** flowers.

Adverb—word that modifies (describes) a verb, adjective, or another adverb

The race car driver sped **quickly** down the track.

Preposition—word which relates a noun or pronoun to other words in the sentence and indicates time or location

In the morning, I work **at** the office. (time) (location)

Conjunction—word that connects two entities, ideas, or sentences

Mary loves the sun, **but** she gets a sunburn outdoors. (two sentences)

Interjection—word expressing surprise or emotion

Wow! You won the lottery!

Complements—words that complete the meaning of a sentence. They can be nouns, pronouns, adjectives, or adverbs.

The car is **dirty.** (adjective)   Wash **it**! (pronoun)
Nancy received her **diploma.** (noun)
The soldiers approached **cautiously**. (adverb)

Appendix B

COUNT AND NON-COUNT NOUNS

Non-count	Countables
geography	mountains rivers lakes deserts
biology	plants animals insects reptiles
history	people places events dates
clothing	dresses suits sweaters coats
music	CDs songs instruments records

Non-count	Countables
pastry	cakes pies puddings donuts
entertainment	movies dances concerts comedies
architecture	domes arches columns buttresses
academia	classes teachers students schools
bad weather	floods blizzards hurricanes thunderstorms

Notice that the non-count nouns are all singular and have no plural while the countables are in the plural form.

Appendix C

PREPOSITIONS

Prepositions are words that relate a noun or pronoun to other words in a sentence. The following is a partial list of common prepositions.

about	because of	beside
with	for	against
to	from	into
by	on	under
after	before	of
through	around	at
towards	in front of	behind

Prepositional phrases are groups of words starting with a preposition and followed by a noun or pronoun, usually indicating **time** or **place.** Look at some of the common phrases for both categories.

Time	Place
during the day	under the sofa
in the evening	behind the desk
after lunch	at the corner
before Friday	over the chair
at midnight	between the walls
by next week	beside the car
from 8 a.m. to 7 p.m.	below the clouds

The ball rolled **under the sofa.**

We sat **in front of the fire** to get warm.

Nancy needs to finish her project **by next Tuesday.**

Appendix D

PRONOUNS

Pronouns are words that take the place of nouns and all their modifiers.

Subject	Direct Object	Indirect Object
Performer	First Receiver: person/thing	Second Receiver: usually person
I you (sing.) he, she it	me you (sing.) him, her, it	me you (sing.) him, her, it
we you (pl.) they	us you (pl.) them	us you (pl.) them

He plays the guitar well.   (subject)

I see **them** over there.   (direct object)

Give **me** the book.   (indirect object)

That book is **hers**.   (possessive)

You see **before you** an artistic masterpiece.   (object of the preposition before)

This is my favorite.   (demonstrative)

Possessive	Object of Preposition	Demonstrative
Ownership	to, for, by, with, before, etc. +	Pointing out
mine yours* his, hers, its	me you (sing.) him, her, it	this that
ours yours theirs	us you (pl.) them	these those

*There are no apostrophes before the "s" for the possessive pronouns.

Appendix E

LINKING VERBS

Linking verbs join the subject and the rest of the sentence. They are followed by adjectives, *not* adverbs. These verbs never take a direct object, but may be followed by a subject complement. The subject never performs the action.

JFK **became** president after the 1960 election. (no action)

The following are common linking verbs. Those followed by an asterisk (*) can also be transitive verbs and take a direct object. Look at how their function changes as you compare them as linking (LV) and action (AV) verbs.

seem	become	be	stay*	remain*	grow*	appear*	feel*
look*	get*	smell*	sound*	taste*	turn*	prove*	remain*

Most people **remained** calm during the hurricane. (LV + adj.)
The guests **remained** at the party until midnight. (AV + complement)

Stay here while I run an errand. (AV)
The soldiers **stayed** alert during the military exercises. (LV + adj.)

The night **grew** colder as the snow fell. (LV + adj.)
Joan **grew** tomatoes, peppers, and onions in her garden. (AV + DO)

My friend just **appeared** out of nowhere. (AV)
Jane **appeared** radiant on her wedding day. (LV + adj.)

Phil **is** director of his company. (LV + noun complement)
They **were** sorry to leave Spain after their wonderful vacation. (LV + adj.)

Marco **seems** excited about his new job. (LV + adj.)
No one **seemed** to care about the outcome of the election. (LV + complement)

The police **sounded** the alarm. (AV + DO)
Mike **sounded** sad after he heard the news. (LV + adj.)

Appendix F

SUBJECT/VERB AGREEMENT

The following are **always** singular:

anybody (thing, one)	either/neither + singular noun
somebody (thing, one)	the number of + singular or plural noun
nobody (thing, one)	gerund as a subject
each	
every	

The following words ending in "s" are **not** plural:

arthritis	chess	tennis	stress
checkers	economics	mathematics	news
measles	mumps	physics	bliss
politics	shingles (disease)		

Some words use the same form for singular and plural, such as:

fish	deer	sheep
moose	reindeer	caribou

The following are **always plural**:

both	people	several
pants	scissors	

Be careful with irregular plurals such as these:

children	geese	lice	men
oxen	people	teeth	feet
mice	women	alumni	bacteria
phenomena	media		

Appendix G

PERFECT TENSES

A simple past tense views the action as completed in the past with no reference to the present. The present perfect, however, views an action begun in the past and possibly repeated up to the present. "The Allens **moved** to Miami in 1990 (completed past action) and **have lived** there since then (repeated to the present)." The timeline indicates whether it is totally completed or repeats itself to the present. Compare the following:

Yesterday I **got up** early, **went** to school, and **took** an exam.

Over and done with at midnight.

This morning I **have awoken** early, **taken** two exams, and **spoken** with several friends.

This morning is not over and I may do other things to add to my list. Since we are viewing this in the present, the verbs have to be present perfect.

◆ Set up a time line to learn the perfect tenses.

X_____ / (simple past)
completed action   last night

Last night I **finished** my term paper.

X_____ / (present perfect tense)
action   now

(Up to this moment) I **have already finished** my term paper.

X_____
1985 completed action   now

Harry **visited** Italy in 1985. (simple past)

____X_____X_____X_____X_____
1985   now

Since 1985 Harry **has visited** Italy four times. (present perfect)

On June 5th I **saw** the movie "Hawaii." (one time, past)

X_____ / (simple past)
action (June 5th)

June 5th ___X___X___X___X___X_____ /
         └────────────⌣────────────┘
         beginning date   now

Since June 5th, I **have seen** five movies.   (present perfect)

◆ When two actions take place, the first is in the **past perfect** (more past) and the second is in the **simple past** (recent past).

___X X X X X X X X X X X X_____
1973   1996

My brother **worked** as a fireman from 1973 to 1996. **(completed past)**

___X X X X X X X X X X X X_____
first action   time or second action
(worked)   (retired)

My brother **had worked** as a fireman before he **retired**.

___X_____
2004

My family **lived** in Boston in 2004. (simple past)

___X_____
└──────────⌣────────┘ 2005   now

Before 2005 my family **had lived** in Boston. (past perfect)

_____X_____
1985

Terry **drove** to Washington in 1985. (one time completed event)

_____X_____X_____X_____X_____
1985   2005

Before 2005 Harry **has driven** to Washington four times. (past repeated events)

◆ To look at past actions related to the present, use this formula:

$$\text{subject} + \begin{Bmatrix} \text{have} \\ \text{has} \end{Bmatrix} + \text{past participle}$$

My cousins **have lived** in Ohio for many years.

Sarah **has completed** all her courses to graduate.

◆ To look at past actions in relation to another past action, use the following:

subject + simple past + subject + had + past participle

Phil **said** that he **had already read** the book.

I **knew** that my friends **had bought** a new house close to town.

◆ Use this formula for creating questions:

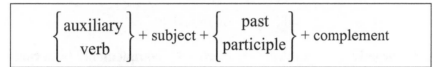

$\left\{ \begin{array}{c} \text{auxiliary} \\ \text{verb} \end{array} \right\}$ + subject + $\left\{ \begin{array}{c} \text{past} \\ \text{participle} \end{array} \right\}$ + complement

Has Louie **finished** writing his project yet?

Had the group **arrived** earlier than expected?

◆ Use this formula for negative sentences:

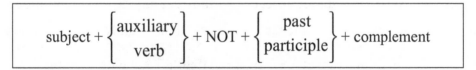

subject + $\left\{ \begin{array}{c} \text{auxiliary} \\ \text{verb} \end{array} \right\}$ + NOT + $\left\{ \begin{array}{c} \text{past} \\ \text{participle} \end{array} \right\}$ + complement

Mary and Bill **have not photographed** the Leaning Tower of Pisa.

The judge **had not rendered** his verdict yet.

◆ Use these formulas for **before** and **after** statements:

subject + had + past participle + **before** + subject + simple past

subject + simple past + **after** + subject + had + past participle

We had **already read** the report before the company **published** it.

My family **moved** to Iowa after my father **had become** CEO of the company.

Appendix H

SENTENCE WORD ORDER

subject + verb + complement
Harry   plays   tennis.

subject + auxiliary + negative + verb + complement
We   do   not   plant   gardens.

auxiliary + subject + verb + complement?
Are   they   talking   on the telephone?

auxiliary + negative + subject + verb + complement? (as a contraction)
Doesn't   the secretary   take   dictation?

subject + verb + direct object + (complement)
The students   take   the bus   to school.

subject + verb + direct object + indirect object + (complement)
Lucy   writes   a letter   to her family   every week.

subject + auxiliary (have) + past participle + complement
No one   has   seen   that new movie yet.

subject + auxiliary + negative + past participle + complement
The teachers   have   not   written   the exams.

subject + auxiliary + adverb + past participle + complement
The plane   has   already   arrived   at the airport.

Appendix I

TAG QUESTIONS

Tag questions are a verification—affirmative or negative—of what the speaker said in the main clause. The tag at the end of the sentence is set off by a comma.

subject + verb, auxiliary + negative + subject ?

subject + auxiliary + negative, auxiliary + subject ?

Remember the following when using tag questions:

◆ If the main clause is affirmative, the tag will be negative and vice versa.

You **speak** Spanish, **don't** you?

Todd **won't** arrive late, **will** he?

◆ The auxiliary verb of the main clause will be the auxiliary of the tag.

can	could	would	should	have	has
will	is	are	was	were	had

There **are** only 28 days in February, **aren't** there?

Sandy **can** dance the tango, **can't** she?

◆ If there is no expressed auxiliary, use **do, does,** or **did.**

The plane arrived late, **didn't** it?

Herman speaks well, **doesn't** he?

◆ Use the same tense in both clauses.

They **went** to the country fair last week, **didn't** they?

Mark **will** drive to San Diego, **won't** he?

◆ A negative tag usually uses the contraction (n't) form.

Ernest won the prize, **didn't** he?

The doctor is in the hospital, **isn't** she?

Appendix J

USE OF ARTICLES *A*, *AN*, AND *THE*

A, an, and *the* are called articles. The first two are indefinite articles because they do not refer to anything specific.

I ate **an orange** for lunch. (It was not a specific orange.)

Give me **a book** (any book) to prop up the projector.

A and *an* can be used to modify only singular nouns. *Some* is the corresponding indefinite article for more than one. *The* is a definite article because it refers to something specific and can be used with either singular or plural.

The red car (specific one) is nicer than **the other two** in the showroom.

Use *a* before a word beginning with a consonant sound:

a house   **a** pencil   **a** boy   **a** wagon

Be careful with words beginning with *H* and *U* because they can have either a consonant or a vowel sound. When you do not know the pronunciation of a word, look it up in a dictionary or ask a native speaker to pronounce it for you. Here are some that have a consonant sound.

helmet	uniform
hint	unicorn
hip	university
house	unique

Words that begin with a vowel (*a, e, i, o*) sound, always require the article *an*.

an apple	**an** aunt	**an** Eskimo
an Indian	**an** elephant	**an** ice cube
an organ	**an** opening	**an** oculus

An exception to the vowel rule occurs when *one* comes before a noun and there is a hyphen between the two. Use *a*, not *an*.

a one-horse carriage	**a** one-act play
a one-armed bandit	**a** one-time offer

However, words that begin with *u* can have a consonant or vowel sound. You need to know how to pronounce the word.

Consonant U (yoo) sound	Vowel U (cŭp)
a universe	**an** umbrella
a unified group	**an** unimportant document
a unit	**an** unpleasant sound

The (YOO) sound can also be spelled with *eu*. Use *a* with these

a European train	**a** eucalyptus tree	**a** eulogy
a euphoric mood	**a** euphemism	**a** Eurail pass

Appendix K

ADVERBS

There are two types of adverbs: **time/location** that do not usually end in *ly*, and **manner**, expressing how an action was undertaken. The latter always ends in *ly*.

These adverbs of time can come either at the beginning or the end of the sentence. If you are stressing the time element, then put it at the beginning. Look at the following:

soon	later	yesterday	last night	never	hardly
late	any time	every day	tomorrow	forever	always

Yesterday it rained hard all day, but last month we had no rain at all.

We had our monthly meeting **yesterday** as usual.

The plane arrived at 5:30. **Later** we ate at the Blue Parrot Restaurant.

I'll see you **later**.

Adverbs that modify other adverbs do so by showing intensity or degrees of carrying out the action. The following are adverbs that modify other adverbs. They come directly before the second adverb.

extremely	much	really*	so	too	very

***Really** is more informal than the others.

Because it was raining **extremely hard**, we had to pull off the road to avoid an accident.

The children were **too tired** to play any more games, so they took a nap.

Tom drove **much more slowly** than usual on the winding mountain roads.

Most words that end in *ly* are adverbs, but some adjectives end in *ly* also. Adverbs are usually formed by adding *ly* to the adjective form. Not all adjectives can become adverbs. Here are some common adjectives that end in *ly*. Notice that they have a noun base. These usually use nouns referring to people, and the *ly* means "like."

friendly = like a friend

friendly	motherly	kingly	homely	queenly
only (one)	priestly	saintly	fatherly	heavenly

With adverbs, however, the *ly* means *how, in what manner*.

Adjectives ending in *l* add *ly*
skillful—skillfully   special—specially   joyful—joyfully

Adjectives ending in *ic*, add *al* + *ly*
angelic—angelically   magic—magically   basic—basically

Adjectives ending in a consonant + *y* change *y* to *i* and add *ly*
merry—merrily   happy—happily

Adjectives ending in a vowel + *y* or one syllable words add *ly*
coy—coyly   shy—shyly   hot—hotly   smart—smartly

Adjectives ending in *ble* change suffix to *bly*
humble—humbly   horrible—horribly   noble—nobly

Appendix L

COMPARATIVES

To show a relationship between two objects, persons, or groups that are equal or unequal to the same element of another object, person, or group, then the comparative is used. Most one- and two-syllable adjectives add *-er* to express unequal comparisons.

Adjective + *er*
Adverb + *er*

quiet > quieter   high > higher   neat > neater

fast > faster   quick > quicker   soon > sooner

Adjectives ending in *e* just add *r* to the root.

Adjectives ending in [*e* + *r*]

nice > nicer   white > whiter

fine > finer   tame > tamer

Adjectives ending in [consonant + *y*] change *y* > *i* before adding *er*

happy > happier   dainty > daintier

pretty > prettier   lovely > lovelier

Adjectives ending in a [vowel + *y*] just add *er*

coy > coyer   gay > gayer (happy)   gray > grayer

Some two-syllable and all three-syllable or more adjectives and adverbs use *more* or *less* adjective or adverb for the comparison.

Less / More } + Three-syllable adjectives

more (less) intelligent   more (less) beautiful   more (less) graceful

more (less) interesting   more (less) agonizing   more (less) skillful

When you compare more than two entities, you take one out of the group and compare it to the remaining entities. The formula for comparisons changes for the *superlative*.

Adjective + *est*

dark > darkest   broad > broadest   clean > cleanest   fresh > freshest

firm > firmest   slow > slowest   narrow> narrowest

Adjectives ending in e add *st*

large > largest   blue > bluest

true > truest   simple > simplest

Adjectives ending in [consonant + *y*] change *y* > *i* before adding *est*

lazy > laziest   curly > curliest

sunny > sunniest   healthy > healthiest

Adjectives ending in a [vowel + *y*] just add *est*

gay > gayest (happy)   gray > grayest

Some two-syllable and all three-syllable or more adjectives use *most* or *least* + the adjective for the superlative.

Least / Most } + Three-syllable adjectives

most (least) understanding   most (least) comprehensive

most (least) careful   most (least) childish

Appendix M

DOUBLING THE FINAL CONSONANT

Verbs that double the final consonant before adding *ed* or *ing*.

One-syllable or two-syllable verbs with a stressed second syllable double the final consonant before adding *ed* or *ing* when the final consonant is preceded by a single vowel.

Infinitive	-s Form	-ed Form	-ing Form
defer	defers	deferred	deferring
drop	drops	dropped	dropping
emit	emits	emitted	emitting
hop	hops	hopped	hopping
jam	jams	jammed	jamming

Adjectives that double the final consonant before adding *er* or *est*.

One-or two-syllable adjectives ending in a single consonant and preceded by a single vowel double the final consonant. Exceptions are words ending in *x* and *w*.

thin/thinner   hot/hotter   sad/sadder   fat/fatter

Verbs that change the *y* to *i* before adding suffixes *s* or *ed*.

Words that end in [consonant + *y*] change the *y* to *i* before adding the suffixes *s* or *ed*. However, when adding the suffix *ing*, they keep the *y* and just add the suffix.

Infinitive	-s Form	-ed Form	ing Form
apply	applies	applied	applying
beautify	beautifies	beautified	beautifying
bury	buries	buried	burying
carry	carries	carried	carrying
classify	classifies	classified	classifying

Glossary

Adjective: word that describes a noun or pronoun.

Adverb: word that modifies a verb, adjective, or another adverb.

Antecedent: word that comes before and is related to another word in the sentence (often a noun in a clause that relates to a pronoun in another clause).

> The **director (**noun antecedent**) whom** (pronoun related to the noun) you met last night will be the guest speaker at today's luncheon.

Agreement: how words correspond to other words in a sentence or phrase.

Capitalization: writing words with a large or capital letter; refer to the section on capitalization.

Clause: part of a sentence; *main clauses* (independent) can stand alone and convey a complete thought. *Dependent clauses* (subordinate) do not convey a complete idea even though they may contain a subject and verb. The latter need the main clause to give the whole structure meaning.

Comma: punctuation mark indicated by the symbol (,) – used to separate elements in a series, to separate complete sentences introduced by *and*, *but*.

Exclamation point: punctuation mark indicated by the symbol (!) – used to express elements of surprise.

> Sharks! Get out of the water!

Fragment: part of a sentence that does not convey a complete idea.

> That morning in the park.

Interjection: a word showing surprise or emotion

> **Wow!** What a beautiful diamond ring she's wearing!

Main clause: in a sentence composed of two clauses, the main clause is the one conveying a complete thought.

Modify: describe

Participle: form of verb usually ending in *ed* (past) or *ing* (present)

        frightened/frightening   fried/frying

Period: punctuation mark using the symbol (.) – used mostly at the end of a declarative sentence.

Preposition: word relating a noun or pronoun to other words in a sentence, such as *in, into, on, to, by*

        The tickets are **for** the afternoon performance.

Question mark: punctuation mark using the symbol (?) – used after an interrogative statement, one in which the speaker asks for certain information.

        When is your friend arriving**?**

Sentence: group of words containing a subject, a verb, and a complete thought.

        Mrs. Davis drove to Chicago on Monday.

Subordinate (dependent) clause: one which contains a subject and a verb, but one which does not convey a complete thought. It depends on the main clause to give it meaning.

        Because it was raining very hard, we were forced to cancel the bicycle races.

        The show had already started, **but** we decided to go anyway.

NOTES

NOTES

NOTES

NOTES

NOTES

NOTES

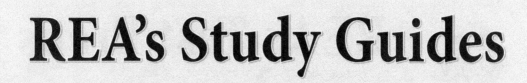

REA's Test Preps
The Best in Test Preparation

- *REA Test Preps are **far more** comprehensive than any other test preparation series*
- *Each book contains full-length practice tests based on the most recent exams*
- ***Every** type of question likely to be given on the exams is included*
- *Answers are accompanied by **full** and **detailed** explanations*

REA publishes hundreds of test prep books. Some of our titles include:

Advanced Placement Exams (APs)
Art History
Biology
Calculus AB & BC
Chemistry
Economics
English Language & Composition
English Literature & Composition
European History
French Language
Government & Politics
Latin Vergil
Physics B & C
Psychology
Spanish Language
Statistics
United States History
World History

College-Level Examination Program (CLEP)
American Government
College Algebra
General Examinations
History of the United States I
History of the United States II
Introduction to Educational Psychology
Human Growth and Development
Introductory Psychology
Introductory Sociology
Principles of Management
Principles of Marketing
Spanish
Western Civilization I
Western Civilization II

SAT Subject Tests
Biology E/M
Chemistry
French
German
Literature
Mathematics Level 1, 2
Physics
Spanish
United States History

Graduate Record Exams (GREs)
Biology
Chemistry
General
Literature in English
Mathematics
Physics
Psychology

ACT - ACT Assessment
ASVAB - Armed Services Vocational Aptitude Battery
CBEST - California Basic Educational Skills Test
CDL - Commercial Driver License Exam
COOP, HSPT & TACHS - Catholic High School Admission Tests
FE (EIT) - AM Exam
FTCE - Florida Teacher Certification Examinations
GED
GMAT - Graduate Management Admission Test

LSAT - Law School Admission Test
MAT - Miller Analogies Test
MCAT - Medical College Admission Test
MTEL - Massachusetts Tests for Educator Licensure
NJ HSPA - New Jersey High School Proficiency Assessment
NYSTCE - New York State Teacher Certification Examinations
PRAXIS PLT - Principles of Learning & Teaching Tests
PRAXIS PPST - Pre-Professional Skills Tests
PSAT/NMSQT
SAT
TExES - Texas Examinations of Educator Standards
THEA - Texas Higher Education Assessment
TOEFL - Test of English as a Foreign Language
USMLE Steps 1,2 - U.S. Medical Licensing Exams

For our complete title list,
visit www.rea.com

Research & Education Association